PRAISE FOR INSIGHTFUL KNOWLEDGE

Stephen Monaco, grand master of guerrilla marketing and one of the true marketing pioneers of the early years of the tech business continues to amaze me. This guy is for real and he did in fact write the book on social media strategy! Whether you are a novice or a self proclaimed expert, buy it! It is very appropriately called, *Insightful Knowledge*.
King R. Lee – President and CEO, Good Technology, Inc.

This book is full of impressively powerful guidance based on real experience and tremendous success. *Insightful Knowledge* will sway doubting executives to the ways of adaptive marketing, persistent listening, and comprehensive voice of customer initiatives. This is one of the best business books written in years!
R. Otto Maly – President & Director of Special Projects, Kroenke Holdings

Stephen Monaco delves deep into the changing landscape of social media, delivering insights into how today's consumers interact with brands across channels. From social networks to social TV, he distills a vast amount of theory into powerful nuggets of marketing strategy. Packed with case studies and practical tips, the aptly named *Insightful Knowledge* is a must read for marketing professionals.
Kerry Gorgone, JD, MBA – Social Media Professor, Full Sail University

We can't market the way we used to. As Stephen Monaco shows us in Insightful Knowledge, if we're not successfully using social media we cannot succeed. Monaco gets us up to speed as quickly as possible. From listening to customers, to measuring, to calculating ROI, Monaco guides us to successfully marketing with social media. Change has already happened; the question is: "Have you adapted?"
Jonathan Peters, Ph.D. – International Persuasive Communications Expert, and Author of *Cavemen Can't Market*

Since 1987, Stephen Monaco has been in the trenches of online communities utilizing the strategies and tactics that now considered best practices for social media marketing to build a global brand. In *Insightful Knowledge,* Monaco generously shares the methodologies he has employed, and I continue to see how these can be implemented to grow my clients' revenues and brand.

John Strosahl – VP of Global Revenue, Digital River, Inc.

I have known Stephen Monaco for 25+ years. He is always on the forefront of market trends. Stephen blends some very important elements in this must read book. He is a marketing pundit, and provides rock solid advice based on his real-world success. *Insightful Knowledge* correctly focuses on business outcomes, and more importantly the bottom line.

Nick Vedros – World Renowned Commercial Photographer, Public Speaker, Founder and CEO, Vedros & Associates

I jumped at the chance to read this book and was rewarded with, as the title says *Insightful Knowledge* and a clearer understanding of the need to understand engagement. If you want to understand how to use the medium for maximum effectiveness, Stephen Monaco provides the why and how on the ins and outs of social media marketing in a straight-forward manner that can be put to use immediately. Reading this book once will not be enough. It will become your reference on how to engage on the Internet in an effective and productive way.

John Butterill – Founder, Virtual Photo Walks

Social media is the most powerful business and marketing tool ever developed. Yet research shows the vast majority of CEOs believe their organizations have only rudimentary knowledge of how to use social media. In my experience, working around the world, I have found no one who has the strategic knowledge of social media marketing that Stephen Monaco has. *Insightful Knowledge* is the social marketing strategy bible, an absolutely essential read for everyone in business.

Bob Pritchard – The Business Leader's Advisor, International Business Speaker, radio host of business talk show; and Best-Selling Author of *Kick-Ass Business & Marketing Secrets: How to Blitz Your Competition*

Stephen Monaco doesn't just talk social media, he lives it! He knows what works and why, and in this book he shares his secrets with you. You can follow one of the top marketing experts on Twitter (which he is!) but why not drink from the fountain itself? Do not pass go without reading *Insightful Knowledge* if you want to be and stay relevant in today's world! What are you waiting for?

Paige Arnof-Fenn – Founder and CEO of the global strategic marketing firm Mavens & Moguls, writer for Forbes

The world of marketing and PR has changed dramatically in just a few years and social media is now the lynchpin in any successful marketer's strategy. In his new book, veteran marketer Stephen Monaco provides a detailed roadmap and handbook to using social media marketing in this digital age, backed up with real-world examples from the trenches.

Alex Eckelberry – Board member, advisor, formerly CEO of Sunbelt Software

Today it seems that everyone claims to be a social expert, but very few offer anything that will provide an "insightful edge." Stephen's book, *Insightful Knowledge* is packed with valuable information about how brands must evolve to engage with consumers directly. He provides a clear guide how to build deep, long-term relations with customers across multiple platforms. Insightful Knowledge is an invaluable guide for those who want to understand how social media evolved to where it is today, and how to utilize the medium for maximum effectiveness.

Danny Gutknecht – CEO and Co-Founder, Pathways TV

Social media is completely transforming marketing and Stephen Monaco provides the excellent road map required to navigate social marketing with precision. *Insightful Knowledge* is a must read for anyone in any aspect of business – from entrepreneurs to CEOs of the Fortune 500. Read this book now!

Dr. David Farnum – Founder and CEO, True North Technologies

There are a lot of so-called "social media gurus" out there, most are really Stephen Monaco wanna-bes! Involved and successful with online communities since the late 1980s, Stephen is <u>finally</u> sharing his real-world, time tested techniques and cutting edge advice, that will propel any mid-sized business to the next level by developing and growing a relevant social media presence. If your brand is important to you, *Insightful Knowledge* gives a thorough understanding of social marketing, its many benefits, as well as how to engage existing clients, and attract many, many more!
Dusty Meehan – Founder and CEO, eLumina Communications

Brilliant! With case studies, real world data, and world-class expertise, Stephen Monaco does more than pontificate about the power of social media. *Insightful Knowledge* lifts the veil to reveal <u>how</u> to strategically use social marketing to create the kind of engaging, purposeful social media presence required for long-term success.
Mindy Audlin – speaker, radio personality, and author of *What If It All Goes RIGHT?*

You can no longer sit back, relax and put your business on auto-pilot when it comes to social media. Creating a marketing calendar of automatic tweets, auto-responders and canned replies is not going to cut it when your competition reads *Insightful Knowledge* and takes their engagement to the next level. Stephen Monaco is right on target with his understanding of social media, and if you don't take his advice be assured your competition will. This is not just another theoretical book. By the end of it, you'll know exactly what you need to do, and how to do it. *Insightful Knowledge* not only gives you the tools, it also teaches you how to use them to create an engaged community around your brand that will not only increase your bottom line, but add the soul factor to the life of your business. Prepare to engage!
Yifat Cohen – G+GoTo Gal

Building an army of fans across social media platforms is one thing. However, developing and maintaining consumers' trust requires *insight*. When it comes time for these highly-engaged fans to make purchasing decisions or talk positively about your product, they're

willing participants because by engaging with them you've earned their loyalty. Stephen's *Insightful Knowledge* provides the principles and ideas to keep your social marketing fresh, relevant and amplified.
Robert E. Elliott - technology marketer & Chief Marketing Officer, Smith Micro Software, Inc.

We thought we knew everything there was to know about social media marketing; however, Stephen Monaco teaches every reader several things, and then some. *Insightful Knowledge* clearly demonstrates how social media marketing levels the playing field so little guys can compete, and illustrates why the bigger players need to pay attention. By using historical case studies to current success stories, Monaco assists you in understanding why you need to have your social marketing game on. Develop, launch, evaluate, monitor and adjust...it is all here. Like it or not, social marketing is now part of our mainstream strategies, and it's in our best interest to become the best at it. If you only read one book on social media marketing, make *Insightful Knowledge* that book. This really is a must read for all entrepreneurs, and the CEOs of any company, of any size.
Ken Johnson – CEO, Thinkubator, Inc.

Totally Awesome! Stephen Monaco offers a comprehensive guide to social media marketing in *Insightful Knowledge*. He changes perceptions on social media marketing and tell readers how to develop their marketing strategies. Since social media needs to be part of your marketing efforts, read this book!
Monica Cornetti – Leading Authority on Entrepreneurial Thinking, and Author of *Your Face Isn't Finished Until Your Lipstick is On*

As we progress further into the digital communications age, everyone from executives to artisans are re-evaluating the way they interact with others online. The information in *Insightful Knowledge* is a true gift from Stephen Monaco to anyone looking to make social marketing a permanent fixture in their corporate or personal brand. No entity is too large or too small for the bounty of information he offers. This book is a must-read for anyone who needs a fresh, game-changing perspective on their marketing strategy.
Chris Sembower – Renowned Designer and Illustrator

Forward by Sarah Hill

insightful
KNOWLEDGE

AN ENLIGHTENED VIEW OF
SOCIAL MEDIA
STRATEGY & MARKETING

STEPHEN MONACO

INSIGHTFUL KNOWLEDGE:
AN ENLIGHTENED VIEW OF SOCIAL MEDIA STRATEGY & MARKETING

Published by Total Publishing and Media, LLC
5332 S. Memorial Drive, Suite 200, Tulsa, OK 74145

Bulk Sales

For bulk orders of this book please contact the author via his website: StephenMonaco.com

ISBN: 978-1-937829-88-9 (paperback)
ISBN: 978-1-937829-63-6 (hardback)
ISBN: 978-1-937829-66-7 (ebook)

1. Internet marketing. 2. Social media – Economic aspects. 3. Online social networks – Economic aspects. 4. Strategic planning. 5. Relationship marketing. 6. Consumer behavior. 7. Customer relations. 8. Customer satisfaction. 9. Word-of-mouth advertising. 10. Branding (Marketing)

Printed in the United States of America

Trademarks

The company, product and service names used in this book are for identification purposes only. All trademarks and registered trademarks, service marks and registered service marks are the property of their respective owners. Use of a term in this book should be regarded as affecting the validity of any trademark or service mark.

Disclaimer of Warranty

While best efforts have been used preparing this book, the author and publisher make no representations of warranties with respect to the accuracy or completeness of this book and specifically disclaim any implied warranties of merchantability or fitness for a particular purpose. No warranty may be created or extended by sales representatives, written or electronic sales materials. The advice and strategies contained herein may not be suitable for your situation, and all information is provided on an "as is" basis. Neither the author or publisher shall be liable for any loss of profit or any other commercial damages, including but not limited to special, incidental, consequential, or other damages.

Cover Illustration

Chris Sembower / ChrisSembower.com

DEDICATION

This book is lovingly dedicated to Michele, Spencer and Shelby.

~ **Stephen**

TABLE OF CONTENTS

CHAPTER 1
What's Past Is Prologue

CHAPTER 2
Sweeping Changes in How Consumers Interact with Media

CHAPTER 3
Internet Use Shifts Power to Consumers

CHAPTER 4
Market Driven Companies

CHAPTER 5
Adaptive Marketing

CHAPTER 6
Developing a Social Media Marketing Strategy

CHAPTER 7
Persistent Listening

CHAPTER 8
Engagement

CHAPTER 9
Conversions, Metrics and Attributions

CHAPTER 10
Brand Advocates

CHAPTER 11
Word of Mouth

CHAPTER 12
Social Media and ROI

AFTERWORD

WHY READ THIS BOOK?

In short, you should read this book to truly understand social media, the strategies and marketing tactics that make up the best practices for successful social media marketing, and all the components interrelated to social marketing initiatives. This book – based on the knowledge I've gained since 1987, will serve as a valuable source of information – providing guidance and perspective to organizations of all kinds.

Whether your company is in the B2C or B2B space, whether you believe it, like it, or are ready for it, social media is the future now, and mastering all aspects of social media marketing is absolutely crucial.

Social media marketing has gone from a "nice to have" to a "must have" – the ability for companies to succeed online is no longer a viable option without it. Social media marketing is essential to your organization's long-term survival. It's that important!

Today's increasingly complex business environment moves at a tempo that continues to escalate. Companies are now faced with challenges they hadn't contemplated just a few years earlier. It's getting harder and harder to keep up with the brisk pace – and with their competitors.

The Special Report published in 2010 by McKinsey & Company, "What Comes Next? 5 Crucibles of Innovation That Will Shape Into the Coming Decade" delves into macro-level transformations unlike anything before – changes that will have long-term consequences for businesses of all shapes and sizes in most industry sectors in this decade, and many years beyond. Interconnectedness is one of these transformations; and as a result, extraordinary social media is absolutely imperative.

The transformations underway require organizations to continually adapt to facilitate one-to-one interplay between brands and consumers. The days of push marketing have waned and given way to strategies that zero in on the formation of exceptional experiences for individual consumers rather than campaigns aimed at target audiences.

This adaptation requires a thorough comprehension and execution of social media marketing. This book serves as an excellent guide. Full of data, trends, facts, statistics, informative case studies, and best practices it provides details regarding the strategic use of social media to reach desired business outcomes that directly coincide with corporate objectives.

The ability to market on a one-to-one basis has been made possible by consumer's immersion in social media and marketer's ability to gain keen insight into consumer sentiments and to interact with them in real-time. To stay in harmony with their public, brands must continuously reinvent or face irrelevance. Irrelevance equals extinction.

Maintaining relevance requires perpetually engaging consumers in meaningful dialogues that result in actual relationships. These relationships help companies better understand not only what consumers want, but what they actually value – enabling insights for making data-driven decisions. This valuable data empowers companies to adapt expeditiously wherever necessary. Companies that don't adapt are going to suffer, and shouldn't be surprised when their customers have become their competitor's customers.

Social media marketing is misunderstood, but it isn't alchemy. It's a component of an integrated marketing mix, albeit increasingly the most important one. It must be utilized strategically along with all the other components like display and digital advertising, public relations, inside sales, outside sales, events, sponsorship, content marketing, inbound marketing, etc.

With all the global changes, increased competition, and the breakneck tempo of business today, organizations must utilize every marketing resource possible, and social media marketing provides tremendous value. Failing to make the most of the component that holds the most promise is like tying one hand behind your back while facing off against competitors. This book will not only provide the necessary illumination to keep companies from fumbling around in the dark, but provide keen perception to successfully execute impactful social media marketing initiatives leading to increases in growth, revenue, and earnings.

ACKNOWLEDGEMENTS

Very special thanks to my wonderful wife Michele, and our awesome children, Spencer and Shelby, my mom, and brother John.

My sincere appreciation goes to a handful of people who provided help while writing this book and to many others who were supportive and inspirational to me whether or not they realized it. My thanks to: Sarah Hill, Tracy Panko, Spiral16, Chris Sembower, Kerry Gorgone, Michelle Mull, Christina Trapolino, Meghan Brindley, Yifat Cohen, Paige Arnof-Fenn, King R. Lee, Bob Pritchard, R. Otto Maly, John Strosahl, Robert E. Elliott, Ken Johnson, Dr. David Farnum, Danny Gutknecht, Jonathan Peters, Ph.D., Monica Cornetti, John Butterill, Dusty Meehan, Alex Eckelberry, Emerick Woods, Michelle Lamar, Eric Melin, Peter Biadasz, Christopher L. Simmons, Brant Brukowsky, Brock Brukowsky, Amy Bader Meier, Todd Meier, Anne McLeod Kelly, Bruce Barkelew, Brad Muhl, Neal Danner, Andrés Silva Arancibia, Evan Carmichael, Nancy Pekala, Dr. Bea Smith, Craig Rogers, Bruce Garber, Terry Dingwall, Barnard Crespi, Rick Kinnard, Laurie DesAutels, Dragana Simic, Angeline Stacy, T. Lee, Brooksie, Anne Fisher, Frank Fisher, Jill Meyer, Brenda McGavock, Ph.D., Laurie Kane, Ph.D., Lynett Rogers, Luciano Cola, Jack L. Shelton, Jennifer Luney, Eric Standlee, Mitchell From, Chrissy Bernal, Richard J. Kane, Jami Conrad Clevenger, Natalie Jobe Mills, Sherrill Stewart Bass, and most importantly thank you to God Almighty.

FOREWORD

"Genius is the very eye of intellect and the wing of the thought; it is always in advance of its time, and is the pioneer for the generation which it precedes."

~William Gilmore Simms

During a television newscast one evening, a new father on the other side of the country hopped in my Google+ Hangout and via his smart phone camera showed me his hours old baby snuggled in his wife's hospital room. Via a social networking site, I watched the newborn's belly go up and down with each breath. This interaction was deeper than a TwitPic, a still photograph on Twitter. It was in real time. I quickly realized our Global Village is no longer just text based. With the prevalence of webcams, we have entered a new layer of real-time social media that is living, breathing... *Human Media.*

In 2011, I thought it might be interesting to use the webcam on a laptop computer to hold a group video chat behind the scenes of our newscasts on KOMU-TV, the NBC affiliate in Columbia, Missouri. June 2011 was the launch of a new social network called Google+ and I decided to try "Hangouts" – which would become the platform's killer app. Over the coming months on that laptop, chatting with viewers during the sound bites and commercials, people around the world flooded in to see everything from microphone checks to our shoes that are usually hidden under the news desk. Our mid-Missouri TV station suddenly had an online global audience that we could see and hear from our news set. The viewers who were once sequestered behind the TV glass suddenly had our eyes and ears. We could see in their living rooms. They could whisper in our ears.

For the first time in my 20 years as a broadcaster, I was able to *see and hear* the audience react to our stories in real-time. It fascinated the heck out of me. I started to wear two earpieces, one for my producer and one for the people in my Google+ Hangout who watched and contributed to our newscasts as a live, virtual studio audience. I'd read a story and I'd hear the audience react in real time. When I'd report a story about a child murder, I could hear the people in the Hangout sigh. I'd mispronounce a word and the viewers in the Hangout would politely correct me in my ear. During a bank robbery, they'd crowd source information using their own social platforms and share it with me face-to-face in real time. Since you can share your computer screen with others during a Hangout, viewers would pull up maps of breaking news event locations. It was as if I had nine additional producers in the studio with me to crowd source information. People started joining my newscast Hangouts from Australia to Zimbabwe despite the fact we were reporting Missouri news. Why? ...because they could *talk* with me not just text with me.

Group video chat rooms like Google+ Hangouts are like magic carpets that can take you around the block or around the world in a matter of minutes. Because Google+ Hangouts live inside a social network, a powerful crowd sourcing tool, television stations and other businesses have the ability to connect with their customers face-to-face in real time. Live tweeting from a news event certainly serves a purpose. "Live Hanging" via video with groups of people from your smart phone is the future.

I felt so passionately about the power of Human Media that I left my job as a broadcaster and went to work for Veterans United, an innovative home loan company that wants to grow its Google+ platform. (google.com/+veteransunited) Here, our Human Media team has developed one of the world's first "Virtual Front Porches" – a face-to-face social endeavor to develop closer relationships with veterans, current service members, and social influencers. Using Google+ as the left hand and YouTube as the right hand, the Veterans United Network (VUN) is using YouTube as a free broadcast tower to share military veterans' stories. VUN is using Hangouts to peel back the corporate curtain and show customers our unique culture as one of the fastest-growing companies in the nation. We are also using Hangouts to educate veterans and current service members about their VA home loan benefit.

Veterans United's volunteer endeavor with Virtual Photo Walks™ also provides World War II veterans who are unable to travel live, virtual video tours of their memorials from Washington, DC to Normandy, France via Google+ Hangouts. Instead of using text-based "handshakes" where veterans could only interact by typing comments, these face-to-face, living, breathing webcam and audio interactions are Human Media hugs. The veterans can ask to move closer to see their war memorials on computer screens, visit with each other in real-time, and talk to the volunteers who are capturing live video and audio on location at their memorials.

During a virtual tour in September 2012, a gentleman who was one of the thousands who stormed the beaches of Normandy as brave teenagers on D-Day in 1944 quietly asked the volunteer with the camera and microphone at Omaha Beach if he would wade out into the sea and turn the camera toward the cliff above the beach. The gentleman wanted to hear the waves as the surf met the sand, and he had the exact vantage point from when he stepped off his landing craft 68 years earlier. I was with the gentleman and his grandson as he sat silently for quite some time and listened to the tranquil waves meet the shore in France from the comfort of his home. I don't know what was going through his mind as he watched and listened, but he was experiencing something powerful and moving: Human Media transported him there.

For 30 minutes each weekday, Veterans United opens a Hangout with no other agenda than to listen, and let people talk about their passions. It was in one of those Hangout listening sessions that

Stephen Monaco and I first met. It was this global magic carpet that can connect two strangers to help them get acquainted and become friends. Stephen is also very passionate about military veterans and is now helping Veterans United get aging and terminally ill veterans into group video chat rooms to virtually tour their memorials. If you know a veteran who is unable to travel, please visit: VirtualPhotoWalks.org to apply for a Veterans Virtual Tour.

After getting to know Stephen, I came to understand how he was a pioneer in literally forming specific online communities to initiate dialogues with consumers to listen and learn about their needs in 1987. Armed with the valuable information provided via direct interactivity with consumers, he oversaw the dissemination of that information across departments throughout his company. The continued utilization of relevant data sets drove the decision making process regarding new product features that precisely met market demands. Stephen also used the very language consumers were using in online communities for marketing communications so advertisements would resonate with the tech savvy audience. In the late 80s, Stephen had already realized the importance of brand advocates and was developing strategies to energize them to drive positive word of mouth to impact consumers' purchasing decisions.

Stephen is a strategic asset with know-how and burning passion – literally an expert in the areas in which he provides guidance. He was using online communities six years prior to the creation of the web browser in ways that are now considered best practices for social media marketing. This was a half dozen years before the World Wide Web even had early adopters, and the term social media was still more than a decade and a half way from being coined. I'm glad Stephen expended the energy to transfer his knowledge into written form, and glad we met in a Google+ Hangout. What a long way online communities have come since the days of the text-based BBS, and CompuServe, to live video tours for aging veterans. Human

Media has reduced the physical space between us and is bringing businesses into face-to-face relationships with consumers to better understand their needs. How? By reading *"Insightful Knowledge"* you'll find out.

Sarah Hill
12-Time Emmy Award Winner
including winning in the "Interactivity" category introduced in 2012
Veterans United Video Storyteller & Hangout Host

INTRODUCTION

Social media is more than marketing communications.

It is more than Facebook, Twitter, Pinterest, and LinkedIn. It is also more than the enabling technologies – wikis, blogs, and social networks. Social media is really about engaging communities in new ways to **achieve** otherwise **impossible business value**. And Stephen Monaco has created a format that makes it easy to take what you already know about your business and your customers and create a plan to use social media to foster a one-on-one relationship with your stakeholders, customers, vendors, and prospects that will support positive returns in all aspects of your business.

If you are looking for a book authored by someone who has been there as a business owner, an entrepreneur, an employee, a leader and strong community advocate with communications and marketing experience – has successfully created marketing strategies and tactics in multiple industries over 25 years – than this is your book.

This book is the only resource you will need to understand what social media means to your business and how to create your personal strategy for implementation to keep your business relevant and develop a more productive relationship with your customers and prospects than you have ever had.

Complete with examples across all industries, written in an easy to understand format and without all the confusing jargon, I have no doubt you will use this book as I am. This book will be a resource kept at my desk and referred back to for many years to come.

With the social media market being over $7B in 2012, yes that is billions of dollars, you should invest ample time creating your customized social media strategy. *Insightful Knowledge* is the tool you need to create that plan.

I understand social media communications can be intimidating. The best way to deal with the trepidation is education. Enjoy this book, Stephen gives you everything you need to create and implement your own social media strategy with confidence.

Tracy Panko
CEO, Spiral16

YOU NEED THIS BOOK IF...

- you don't know where to start with your social media initiatives

- you've started your social media initiatives but aren't sure if you're on the right track

- your social media initiatives are in place and you believe you're on the right track

- none of your social media initiatives are directly tied to specific business objectives

- you fail to use social media monitoring / listening platforms in your social media

- you don't know what consumers are saying about your brand online

- you don't have a comprehensive *Voice of Customer* program in place

- you're not engaging consumers with relevant content across multiple platforms

- your company is driven by sales, rather than by marketing

- the breakneck tempo of today's business makes it difficult to adapt and keep up with change you no longer know how to reach potential customers

HOW THIS BOOK IS ORGANIZED

CHAPTER 1 Social media and online communities have existed much longer than most people realize.

CHAPTER 2 Enormous changes in how consumers interact with media led us to where we are today.

CHAPTER 3 Consumer use of the Internet and social media networks transferred all the power away from media conglomerates, companies, and brands, and put consumers in control.

CHAPTER 4 Why it's necessary for companies to be market driven, and why this model leads to success.

CHAPTER 5 An organizations' need to continually learn, adjust and adapt to be successful with social media marketing.

CHAPTER 6 Developing social media marketing strategies that are in sync with organizational objectives.

CHAPTER 7 Listening, social media monitoring, obtaining pertinent data from the social web, and helpful case studies.

CHAPTER 8 Practical advice on engaging consumers in meaningful dialogues via social media and real world examples of best practices.

CHAPTER 9 Conversions through social media marketing initiatives, metrics, attributions, and measuring information germane to your organization.

CHAPTER 10 Importance of brand advocates, strategies to identify and energize them, and returns provided by brand advocacy.

Chapter 1

WHAT'S PAST IS PROLOGUE

Social Networks and Online Communities Have Been Around For Years

While they're certainly all the rage, social networks and online communities are not new.

Anaïs Saint-Jude, the director of the BiblioTech program at Stanford University in Palo Alto, California claims social networking began in the 1600s as Europeans were inundated with a flood of new modes of communication and experienced information overload. The rapid and continuous exchange of new information being disseminated in 17th century Paris was like the eruption of conversations similar to those on Facebook, Twitter, Google+ and smartphones in the early 21st century.

The Scientific Revolution of the 16th and 17th centuries postulated Earth was not the center of the galaxy. New ideas and knowledge in physics, astronomy, biology, medicine and chemistry brought about the transformation of medieval and ancient views of nature – paving the way for groundwork which led to modern science. Along with the sailing expeditions to the New World and wide spread adoption of Gutenberg's printing press with movable type, there was a lot of new information. People were trying to keep up with the plethora of newfound knowledge and what others had to say about it.

Rather than merely servicing government officials, the use of the postal service increased dramatically and was utilized for transporting communication among the private sector. The number of people writing and responding to letters multiplied rapidly making it difficult to keep up with the pace of writing 15-20 letters daily. Does this sound like a precursor to the e-mail in your Inbox?

An Early Form of Twitter in the 17ᵗʰ Century?

Stanford's Anaïs Saint-Jude refers to this time of "hyper writing" as a period when writing became an addiction of sorts. What types of things were people saying? Similar to the postings on Facebook and Twitter today, many of these writings were comprised of drivel. Rather than writing letters, Parisians anonymously wrote notes criticizing the French government on small bits of paper and tossed them into the street. At one point the streets of Paris were literally filled with small pieces of paper containing scandalous blurbs and political insults written by people who scattered them for the public to read. "Did you hear about Jean-Jacques? LOL!" The brief messages written by unidentified people on these small pieces of paper evaded inspection by the government and became an effective method for coordinating civil disobedience.

This was a very early form of socially networking. Now skip forward a few centuries or so to early forms of online communities and how I became so involved with them.

Data Communications Software

Prior to the dawn of the World Wide Web in 1993, getting online to a BBS, AOL, CompuServe, GEnie, Prodigy, etc., required a personal computer, a telephone line, a modem, and data communications software. A person couldn't dial-in with their modem to get online without data communications software, and ProComm was the de facto standard in the data communications software niche.

While we were undergraduate students at the University of Missouri during the early '80s, my best friend, Bruce Barkelew a computer science major, was working on his own software program – the program that eventually became ProComm. A few years after graduation and employed as a programmer at a Silicon Valley company, ProComm was developed into a very robust data communications program that was ready for primetime. Shortly after Datastorm Technologies, Inc. was founded in 1986, Barkelew asked me to join the company. Deciding to go the entrepreneur route I resigned from my account executive position with the agency in Dallas, relocated, and assumed my new role as the VP of Sales & Marketing and co-CEO. I was heavily involved with the formation and oversight of online communities for ProComm and have remained involved with them ever since.

Based on revenue over the previous five years, in 1992 Datastorm Technologies, Inc. was listed as one of the fastest-growing companies in the United States on Inc. Magazine's "Top 500" list. Datastorm's data communications program ProComm was consistently ranked by PC Magazine in their Top Retail Software list of the 15 best-sellers. ProComm Plus for Windows reached the #1 spot in 1993 and became a global brand published in 11 languages. It remains the world's best-selling PC data communications software of all time.

Bulletin Board Systems

In the early 1980s the Bulletin Board System (BBS), dedicated computers ran software that allowed users access to login over a standard telephone line using a modem and data communications software with terminal emulation capabilities. Upon logging in users uploaded and downloaded software programs, files, and data; read news, bulletins, and exchanged messages with other users on public message boards. BBS' with multiple phone lines typically had "chat rooms" where users interacted with each other in online communities. Playing online video games and competing in real-time against other users was another popular activity on Bulletin Board Systems.

Early on the majority of BBSes were run free of charge by hobbyists – the system operator, (or "SysOp"). Some BBSes charged their users a subscription fee for access to their system to cover costs of the host computer and multiple in-coming phone lines. Eventually companies set up BBSes with a dedicated phone number as a method of supporting and corresponding with their customers. ExecPC, and The Whole Earth 'Lectronic Link, (normally shortened to The WELL), were extremely popular Bulletin Board Systems that rivaled online information services like CompuServe. Bulletin Board Systems were the predecessors to commercial subscription-based "online information services" like CompuServe, GEnie, Prodigy, AOL, the World Wide Web and today's social networks.

Online Communities

AOL, CompuServe, GEnie, Prodigy and similar online information services were not websites, but self-contained networks. The term "social networks" had yet to be coined, but that's what these online information services were. Other than having to dial-in with a modem to connect to online information services, they were paid services and people had to subscribe to access the content. There was no talk of "user generated content" either, but there was plenty of that as well. Including software titles to download for trial like the programs c|net's site, download.com makes available today.

One of the very cool things about online communities when they began remains the same today: the ability to make new acquaintances and interact with like-minded people all over the world to discuss any number of topics in real-time. The advent of the "global village" made the world seem much smaller; connecting and collaborating with people everywhere was embraced with enthusiasm. Datastorm's print ad for ProComm Plus for Windows called, "Totally Connected" visually depicted the global village and was very well received by the public.

CompuServe

CompuServe, (CompuServe Information Service – often referred to by the acronym CIS), was initially founded in 1969 as Compu-Serv Network, Inc. in Columbus, Ohio. In 1975 it began being publicly traded on NASDAQ with the ticker symbol, CMPU. The company changed their name to CompuServe Incorporated in 1977 and was acquired in 1980 by Kansas City, Missouri-based H&R Block. The company's acceptance in the market began to grow steadily. In 1986 CompuServe entered the international arena with its expansion to Japan.

As CompuServe gained popularity they introduced moderated discussion Forums – early forerunners to the countless discussion sites on the web today. Many of these Forums were utilized by software companies as an alternative means for offering customer support to their installed user base. My company, Datastorm Technologies, Inc., staffed a CompuServe Forum to support our very popular data communications software program, ProComm. In the ProComm Forum, Datastorm engaged in one-to-one and one-to-many dialogues with consumers.

By the early 1990s, CompuServe became extremely popular and boasted over a half million paid subscribers visited literally thousands of separate discussion Forums. The enormous variety of topics with a dedicated Forum significantly expanded the audience from one primarily comprised of business users and "techno-geeks" to one that appealed to the masses. The broad range of Forums devoted to entertainment, sports, politics, current events, and hundreds of hobbies and special interests, as well as e-commerce and online multiplayer games attracted the general public in masses.

GEnie

In October 1985, GEnie was founded in Rockville, Maryland and was introduced as a dial-up, text-based commercial online service by the Information Services division of General Electric, (now GXS). GEnie was well-received and gained attention as the first serious commercial competitor to CompuServe.

Similar to the Forums on CompuServe, GEnie's RoundTables were contained message boards which were online discussion areas where people could hold asynchronous conversations in the form of posted messages; chat rooms for real-time text conferences, and a Library for the permanent storage of files. GEnie was an instrumental part of the early online community culture predating the web's emergence as a mass medium. Similar to our association with CompuServe, Datastorm Technologies, Inc. had a formal relationship with GEnie and an online community dedicated to support and engage with ProComm customers, fans, followers, and enthusiasts.

Prodigy

The commercial pay-based online information services market was maturing and by 1990 Prodigy had 465,000 subscribers – second only to CompuServe's 600,000. Prodigy's subscribers had access to a wide variety of networked services, including news, weather, banking, stocks, travel, shopping, bulletin boards, games, polls, expert columns, and an assortment of other features.

America Online

America Online began in 1983 as a company called, Control Video Corporation with a single product offering – an online service called GameLine for the Atari 2600. In October 1989 the service's name was changed to America Online which included classic and casual online games in its product mix. America Online differentiated their offerings by catering to "gamers" with innovative online games.

The company was known as AOL in 1991 and positioned itself as the online service for the growing masses of Americans who were novices about personal computers. This was in stark contrast to CompuServe, which had been serving the technical community for years. In February of that year AOL was launched for DOS – AOL for Windows followed in 1992.

The Web Browser and Advent of the World Wide Web

In 1993 the Mosaic web browser was introduced by the National Center for Supercomputing Applications (NCSA) at the University of Illinois Urbana-Champaign. This was the beginning of the eruption in web use.

Spyglass licensed the technology and trademarks from NCSA for producing their own web browser but never used any of the NCSA Mosaic source code. Subsequently Datastorm Technologies, Inc. licensed Spyglass Mosaic, modified it, and built the web browser Web Zeppelin into ProComm Plus for Windows.

One-to-One

Online communities are useful for communicating with many people at once, or engaging in a one-to-one dialogue; not only between individuals, but between an organization and an individual. In 1997 I began intensely researching the feasibility of using the Internet to build not just relationships via one-to-one marketing but social communities – and contemplating individual customer's experiences.

In 1998 I launched Evolve Internet Marketing (now Evolve Adaptive Marketing) to create e-commerce sites allowing personalized customer experiences for unique users and one-to-one marketing. Evolve's solutions made very strategic use of the Internet – fostering a high level of interaction with customers and providing enriching online experiences. Later that year Evolve created initial web presence for the popular extreme sports apparel company No Fear – including their e-commerce store and online community, "The Void." In 1999 I co-founded iZoom.com, an online community for automotive enthusiasts of all types. I served as iZoom's Chief Internet Officer in Tempe, Arizona.

From Online Communities to Social Networks

GeoCities was an early online community that got underway in mid-1995 and was purchased by Yahoo in January 1999. By June 2002 the social media network Xanga had an estimated 100,000 users and was receiving a million hits a day in traffic. LinkedIn launched in May 2003 followed by Specific Media LLC's introduction of MySpace in August 2003. Facebook went live in February 2004 and Yelp followed in October of that year. Reddit which is a social media news site that's essentially a Bulletin Board System featuring a collection of entries submitted by its registered users was founded in June 2005. Twitter was introduced in July 2006. Pinterest launched as a closed beta in March 2010 and Google+ became open for public use in June 2011.

The term "social media" generally refers to using Internet-based technologies to turn communication into an interactive dialogue, and the introduction of user generated content via low-cost publishing platforms. However, user generated content was normal on BBSes during the mid-1980s. Social media is a term we adopted, yet the term is a misnomer in many ways. A recent Google search on "social media" returned 632 million results. Social media has become a catch-all term for everything from Facebook to FourSquare, LinkedIn to YouTube, Flickr to Reddit, MeetUp to StumbleUpon, Blogger to Vimeo, Google+ to Groupon, Twitter to Tumblr, and Words With Friends to Yelp.

Social Media to Social Media Marketing

Social media has made a tremendous economic impact and changed the rules of engagement for marketing forever. Marketing executives face new challenges as the old tried and true methods are rapidly fading away. Marketing through social media is the future now – companies and brands must adapt – quickly!

Chapter 2

SWEEPING CHANGES IN HOW CONSUMERS INTERACT WITH MEDIA

How We Arrived Where We Are Today

In order to know where things are going it's important to understand how we went from where we were, to where we are today. While they didn't set out to create revolutionary changes, The Millennial Generation, (also referred to as "Generation Y"), had everything to do with life as we now know it. If you weren't born between 1981 and 1994, you aren't part of the Millennial Generation. Although, you're probably going to be very interested to see how your behavior has changed over the last handful of years, and how the gaps between Generation X and the Baby Boomer generations have been bridged by a charge led by Millennials. No matter what age you are, you're likely to be nodding your head as you read parts of this chapter while thinking, "That's me, alright..."

Young Americans: Multitasking and Connected

This generation was born during a time of rapid advances in computer technology and has always been surrounded by electronic devices. Millennials have never experienced life without wireless television remote controls or computers, and are accustomed to having access to vast amounts of information via a few clicks. As a result they are not the least bit patient and they flourish on instant gratification. Due to their impatience and constant need for "speedy satisfaction," they thrive on dealing with many tasks simultaneously and feel that multitasking is an effective and sensible use of their time. They become agitated when they feel their time is being wasted. For instance, they detest doing anything they feel is an unproductive use of their time, like waiting in a queue.

Millennials have grown up in a fast-paced lifestyle full of technology, and are well known for being highly technically literate. They are at ease with speed and change. They want to learn new things very quickly and then move on to the next thing. They are interested in processes and services that work and speed up their interactions. Millennials use technology constantly to maintain relationships. Their focus is on relationship building and maintaining a social fabric. This group sustains a multitasking lifestyle and relies on SMS text messaging, mobile phones and social networking Internet sites like Facebook. Social networking sites have evolved and skyrocketed from a niche activity into an enormous happening that connects literally tens of millions of Internet users. Millennials yearn for a sense of belonging.

Millennials spend nearly 15 hours a day interacting with various media and communications technology. These young people tend to be connected to the Internet or connected to one another 24 hours a day / seven days a week, and they love constant interactivity. They are productive communicators who love to and expect to continually remain in contact whenever they want and wherever they are. Fifty-nine percent of Millennials spend at least an hour a day talking on their mobile phones. Using the term multitasking to describe the Millennials' behavior does not begin to do them justice.

Their Brains Are Wired Differently

In addition to the tremendous amount of media Millennials consume, research has indicated their upbringings in atmospheres permeated with technology caused their brains to be "wired differently." Millennial participants in eye-tracking studies (to determine mind processing speeds) revealed that these youths assimilate information up to five times faster than older adults. Millennials' minds are quite active and productive. Since they are able to take in and absorb information so rapidly, they yearn for multifaceted forms of communication – straightforward interactions tend to bore Millennials very quickly. As a result they expect real complexity from the media they consume – multitasking is hardwired into the Millennials' brains (they rarely focus on one thing at a time). They don't see the efficiency in having their focus on one thing at a time.

Media Consumption in America

In late 2004 the average American spent 10.3 hours per day consuming media. While this was an increase of an hour a day from five years earlier, the amount of media consumption by the average American pales in comparison to the consumption of media by Millennials. The voracious rate in which Millennials consume media is without precedence. Many Millennials now consume the equivalent of an astonishing 11 hours of media within a time span of just six hours. While media consumption is approaching the saturation point, multitasking has increased. The additional time Millennials spend on the Internet is coming at the expense of the time they are spending with more traditional media. Unlike any previous generation their childhood activities were scheduled – they are products of very structured environments. As a result Millennials don't like to spend time sitting idly. This is viewed as a waste of time and causes them to feel restless. To "get productive" this group chooses technology as their method for instant gratification and to "get connected."

Millennials Led the Charge; The Rest of America Was Right Behind Them

Millennials are the generation that changed media. They are comfortable on all platforms and use social networking all the time. It's not uncommon for Millennials to utilize four or five devices and several applications simultaneously. While they are passively watching TV, they're often sending text messages and playing Words With Friends or Draw Something on their smart phones. They are also on their laptops or iPads posting tweets, or on Facebook while looking at videos they find interesting or amusing on YouTube.

In fact studies have shown these youths are spending larger amounts of time using electronic media – they are packing the equivalent of 8.5 hours of media exposure into those 6.5 hours. Cramming an additional two hours of media exposure into the same amount of actual time was a result of the media-hungry Millennials behavior of "media multitasking." They don't just sit down to watch a TV show with their friends or family. They listen to iTunes, watch a DVD, and send text messages to friends all at the same time. They simultaneously absorb other forms of media while watching TV, listening to music, using the computer – even while reading.

Americans Take Control of Their Media Experiences

Millennials thrive on instant gratification. As products of their "always on" environment, they insist on controlling all aspects of their media experience. Generally, they tend to lack patience, abhor the idea of wasting time, and despise any disruption to activities that are not relevant to them or that they cannot immediately control or turn off. This generation demands efficiency and they seek structure simply because there are a lot of things they want to do online. They don't want to waste time.

Ignoring or turning off media that isn't relevant is a trend that now pervades Americans in all age groups. Hence people's need to be in complete control of their media experiences. Unlike other forms of media, the Internet enables us to have the independence and the control we now insist upon. People are becoming much more accustomed to getting the information they want within seconds of deciding they want it. For example, the idea of tuning into the evening television news broadcast to see the local weather forecast is increasingly foreign. Instead they simply use a free weather app on their smartphone or mobile device; or go to Weather.com to instantaneously obtain all the relevant information they desire.

Co-founder of Apple, the late Steve Jobs was known to describe the difference between television and the World Wide Web as, "the difference between lean-back and sit-forward media." Jobs contended that computers networked via the Internet tend to make users lean in, focus and engage, while television encourages people to "zone out." Americans don't exactly zone out while watching television. A much more accurate assessment is that the time they spend watching television is also time spent multitasking and concurrently consuming other forms of media.

Multiple Screens, No Problem

Americans are less mindful of the various different channels of media. Going through a period of media convergence, increased multitasking, and the continuous bombardment of information requires processing copious amounts of content. It's easy to forget if the channel relevant information was received via e-mail, a phone conversation, a text message, a post they saw on Facebook, or a television program. People's minds are very busy; perpetually skimming information and filtering out anything that isn't relevant or interesting to them. While there is a propensity for Americans to keep themselves open to being constantly barraged with information, there is no real line of demarcation regarding from which specific medium the information was received. Information comes via (nearly) continuous streams from websites, social networks, podcasts; terrestrial, Internet, and satellite radio; text messages, Instant Messages; "moving video" via television, sites like YouTube, Vimeo and Hulu; game consoles, online game sites, smartphones and mobile devices.

People Value Integrity

The majority of Americans value integrity and authenticity. However, they simply do not associate integrity with the authoritative-sounding "talking heads" who deliver news, information, advertising, or brand messages via the screens on their televisions or mobile devices. Americans have become accustomed to instant access, rapidly adopted social media networks, and enjoy having access to innumerable sources of information. They take pleasure in opportunities to explore, learn about issues, products and services from other people, digesting the information, and reaching their own conclusions. It's evident by the behavior demonstrated online that Americans are beyond leery about what is being disseminated to them by appointed spokespeople at conglomerate-owned media outlets, corporations, and brands.

Chapter 3

INTERNET USE SHIFTS POWER TO CONSUMERS

Consumers Want Authenticity

Americans as a whole have less trust than ever before in corporations, in main stream media, and in the government. At the time of this writing the approval rating of the United States Congress was abysmally low with a percentage in the single digits; polls indicate Americans are frustrated by the lack of transparency in government. People are tired of being lied to by conglomerates that put profits ahead of consumer's safety and well being. Increasingly large numbers of people rely on blogs and trusted members of their social networks for news and information because of bias in the news media outlets owned by giant corporations with self-serving agendas. Authentic, objective investigative journalism has become a thing of the past. The utilization of blog sites and micro-blog sites like Twitter by people everywhere has brought about a profound change in the way information is rapidly disseminated, and this is dramatically shaping the future of news. This phenomenon is by no means just an American trend. Real-time information and photographs documenting the uprisings in Egypt and Libya during 2011 (which came to be known as "The Arab Spring") were spread instantaneously around the world through tweets and retweets via smartphones.

Swift Changes in Consumer Behavior

While emulating younger siblings, children and grandchildren was not a conscious collective movement, the end result is the same – the general population in America has followed Millennials by openly embracing social media networks. Americans of all ages are becoming digital junkies. In fact consumer behavior has shifted dramatically as millions of people make intensive use of digital devices. Almost 50 percent of American consumers who are online have become advanced users of social networks and smartphones – an increase of over 40 percent from 2008 to 2012.

This growth is a result of advanced use of multiple digital platforms to obtain rich media and content. Men tend to be early adopters of new technologies and devices, women are spending more time on social networks, while consumers overall are spending considerably more time engaging in video content via the Internet.

Social Media Networks: Communications Portals

Social Networks have materialized into the foremost channels of digital communications. They have been the favored channel for people under the age of 35 for a number of years dislodging e-mail, instant messaging, and phone calls. The use of social networks by people 55 and older is growing at a staggering rate; one of every four Americans who are 65 or older are social networkers. Social networks have emerged as the gateway for people to search for photos, videos, and user-generated content posted by their friends. One-third of Americans online use social networks to steer their way to find content on the web. Even though search engines, (especially Google) remain the primary method for the way to find and retrieve online content, the use of social networks to discover new information is growing at a brisk pace. The more time consumers spend online, the more their buying decisions are influenced by friends and other members of social networks.

Smartphones Have Become Multi-Purpose Devices

The ever-increasing processing power of smartphones and the faster speed of wireless data networks has multiplied the use of these mobile devices – they are no longer just cellular phones with features – mobile phones and mobile tablets have assailed the niches of devices like game consoles, portable media players, and even personal computers.

Mobile devices are becoming the preferred device for e-mail, browsing the web, and conducting research to make buying decisions. Over 30 percent of smartphone users choose it for browsing the web even when they're in close physical proximity to their personal computers.

The results from a recent survey conducted by Yahoo and Razorfish revealed of the American adults who responded to the survey, 80 percent of them multitask on their mobile devices while watching their favorite shows on TV, and 70 percent do so on a weekly basis. Nearly half, (49 percent) multitask daily, and 15 percent always multitask remaining on the mobile web via their mobile phone or mobile device for the full duration of the time they spend watching their favorite television shows. These people are texting, talking, sending e-mail, logged into social network sites and sending instant messages – not while their TV is on in the background – but while seated in front of their TVs.

Changing Media Landscape Enabled Consumer Control

Prior to the advent of the World Wide Web in 1993, only a finite number of television networks, magazines, newspapers and radio stations existed; and almost all of these mediums were supported financially by advertising. Clearly advertisers and corporate sponsors were far more concerned with obtaining their own objectives and delivering their messages to target audiences. Mass media conglomerates had very little actual regard for the types of programming American consumers would find most appealing. Even as the number of cable TV stations and vertical market magazines increased (other than traditional mass media) consumers had few alternatives for low-cost entertainment and information. They simply paid attention to the content that was being shoved at them by mass media.

Between 2001 and 2006 consumer's habits with media changed remarkably. Time spent with broadcast television, music and newspapers declined by over 10 percent; yet the time they spent on the Internet increased by an amazing 400 percent. The adoption of the Internet skyrocketed after 2006. Millions of websites available to consumers gave them considerably more control over their media experience. The collective attention span of Americans keeps getting shorter, and their media consumption activities are no longer passive. Enormous audiences of people are no longer readily available to the major broadcast television networks or the brands advertising on them; those days are over. Consumers have seized the day. This vivid change in mass media's landscape has provided millions and millions of communications channels via the Internet, including high-quality programming produced by a multitude of professional and recreational content providers. These factors, combined with the array of devices in which consumers use to connect to the Internet – including desktop and laptop computers, netbooks, tablets like the Apple iPad and those running on Google's Android platform, like Amazon's Kindle, video game consoles with broadband access connected to enormous high-definition flat screen displays, and smart mobile phones have placed consumers in a very stable and irreversible position where they are clearly in charge of their media experiences.

Consumer's Use of the Internet Has Changed

As the Internet gained popularity and became main stream, its use by the American populous has changed dramatically. What's different is the way people are consuming media. In addition to spending more time online than watching TV, an increasing number of people are using the Internet as the hub of their media activity – it has become the medium from which all their other media consumption decisions are made. With the Internet being used as the primary medium, other forms of media are either demoted to an ambient role in the background, or used to aid in guiding other online experiences. At the center of their experiences people across a wide range of ages can be found deeply immersed in online social networks seeking contextual content.

Meet the New Boss

Smart marketers readily acknowledge the fact consumers have already taken the proverbial high ground.

Consumers are the new boss in the media industry. Increasingly they systematically reject the information, entertainment and marketing messages deemed irrelevant. This is forcing programming executives at media conglomerates and brand managers at marketing companies to face a particularly difficult challenge.

The amount of time consumers spend on social networking, and on sites comprised of user generated content like YouTube and Vimeo pose bona fide threats to the institutional power of media companies and the major brands they rely on for advertising revenue. Clearly these huge corporations must figure out how to reinvent their offerings to be centered on increasingly selective consumers since the power has shifted away from the conglomerates over to we the people.

250 Channels and Nothing on TV

Media companies need to get creative fast, figure out how to engage consumers, provide them with relevance, and produce results. With the consumers now in control, media conglomerates and marketing companies alike must gain insight into their behavior and tendencies.

I'm betting against the media conglomerates to figure it out on their own in time to save themselves. Early in my career I worked in marketing for one of the world's largest media companies at their corporate headquarters in Burbank, California. These lumbering giants are quite bureaucratic and aren't nimble enough to get out of their own way, let alone become consumer-centric and market driven. Their best chance for long-term survival is via acquisitions. The Hangouts feature on Google+ offers free third-party applications that enable most anyone to operate like a television station and upload their video content directly to YouTube without spending any money. Besides a computer and a high-speed Internet connection, the only thing needed is a web camera. All the technological "heavy lifting" on the back end is handled by Google; YouTube's parent company.

There are over four billion hours of video content on YouTube; and between 48-72 hours of new content is added every 60 seconds. Every month this Internet video site has over 800 million unique visitors. And since 2011 YouTube receives more than one trillion views annually – that's about 140 views for every person on earth! Clearly there's certainly no shortage of content, and this data doesn't even contemplate the video content available on similar Internet sites.

Internet Video Poised to Usurp Traditional Television

The swell of digital platforms has changed video-viewing habits of consumers as well. Nearly 70 percent of Americans who are online now use their personal computers to view videos, while 33 percent of smartphone users watch videos on those devices. The percentage of online Americans who view Internet content on their televisions has tripled since 2009, and a quarter of these people utilize their television as a device to merely display Internet content they receive via Internet-enabled game consoles, DVR set-top boxes, and DVD players. These individuals are 1½ times more inclined than the general populace to cancel their cable or satellite paid television service, and 75 percent of them are dissatisfied with the offerings from their pay-TV service provider.

Social TV

While there's no standard definition to the embryonic and rapidly evolving industry niche called Social TV, the term is used to describe technologies and processes enabling consumers to connect and engage with creators and distributors of video content as well as other fans. Most media industry analysts agree Social TV pertains to social media activity on traditional televisions, personal computers, mobile devices, and tablet computers. In 2010, the MIT Technology Review listed Social TV as one of the Top 10 most important emerging technologies. Some media industry analysts predict Social TV will be a $12 billion market by 2020, and other analysts believe the $12 billion figure is too low.

Regardless of whether the financial predictions are high or low, the following data is factual. At the end of 2012, the 180+ million Americans who are online will average nearly 23 hours of watching videos online per month. That's equals almost one full day of each month watching videos on sites like YouTube!

Consumers Are Dispersed Amongst Highly-Fragmented Groups

The result of how consumers use online social networking sites, smartphones, and mobile devices has caused a shift in power away from long-established media and marketing companies. The changes in consumer behavior have eroded traditional marketing channels and subsequently fragmented consumers into much smaller splintered groups.

Since consumers are no longer concentrated in a specific media sector, they are elusive and much harder for marketers to target because of the fragmentation of the audience across multiple platforms via a wide variety of devices. This has not been good news for marketers that have relied on traditional methods to reach their "target audience" for decades. However, there is an upside to this emergent set of circumstances. The highly-interactive nature of the Internet's media platforms enables marketers to engage consumers with relevant content and messages via two-way exchanges across multiple platforms.

The TiVo-ization of television followed by the proliferation of content available via the Internet and smartphones has left marketers scrambling to find the audiences that were once relatively easy to target. The proclivity for consumers to create and disseminate user-generated product reviews has produced considerable competition for consumers' attention, and developed into a legitimate force to be reckoned with by the marketers whose old school advertising methods are no longer effective.

Marketers must develop methods for engaging consumers. The exponential growth and fragmentation of new media combined with long-established media environments that are increasingly congested with commercial messages, has resulted in consumers counting on their friends and other influencers as their most trusted resources for making buying decisions. Social networks are extremely productive and well within reach. Adaptive marketers are able to leverage the "social bubbles" within social networks for gaining access to consumers – generating awareness and building credibility with their brand. Prior to attempting to penetrate online social networks savvy marketing executives must be agents of change, knock down silos in the organizations, buck the status quo, and transform their companies to become market driven.

Chapter 4

MARKET DRIVEN COMPANIES

Why Companies Should Be Market Driven

Way too many companies maintain an antiquated mentality and are still driven purely by sales, instead of changing their focus to one driven by marketing. It's baffling to me why sales driven companies remain as such, and maintain their short-term approach when they could be systematically transitioning their organization's culture into one that embraces the concept of being market driven.

Why should a company be "market driven?" Market driven companies surpass their rivals by developing superior levels of ability across the areas of total customer satisfaction, loyalty, research, pricing, product development, distribution channels, promotion, and market management.

How do you know if your company is driven by marketing or sales?

Hint: If popular song titles from the corporate hymnal are, "Smiling and Dialing," and "Churn 'Em and Burn 'Em," it's a safe bet that your company is completely driven by sales.

Another sure sign is if the company's sales team can't stop talking about their latest product or service offerings long enough to listen and learn about their customer's needs. Sales personnel are constantly in touch with existing and prospective customers – these dialogues should be an excellent source of determining customer needs.

Sales Driven Companies Focus on Short Term

Companies driven by sales focus primarily on acquiring customers, grabbing market share, achieving immediate revenues, and controlling costs. They concentrate heavily on increasing short-term ROI which isn't necessarily bad, since consumers always have needs that must be satisfied, and those needs create opportunities for peddlers. However, over the long haul organizations driven by sales grapple with differentiating themselves from their competitors in any way other than pricing – which then becomes their main marketing tactic. While companies who operate their businesses may reduce short-term risk, this method does nothing in the way of developing offerings that carry on – that makes long-term success an uphill battle.

Case Study: Sales Driven Company

An extreme example of a company completely sales driven is a consulting firm based in the Chicago area.

The consulting firm targets businesses by using hundreds of aggressive telemarketers who are compensated on straight commission and are required to make 40 calls per hour to set appointments. High pressure sales tactics are used to offer small business owners an initial evaluation of their business for a nominal fee ranging from $300 to $2,500. The telemarketers are compensated for each appointment they set – the appointment is assigned to a sales associate. Like the telemarketers, sales associates and consultants have a contract labor relationship with the company and all compensation is performance-based. All contract laborers are required to sign non-disclosure agreements with an onerous liquidated damages clause in the case of a breach.

Once on site for the initial analysis, we find the sales associates who use business cards with impressive sounding job titles use memorized scripts taught during training: *to convince small business owners their companies are in serious financial trouble and will fail if they do not immediately retain the services of their firm's "expert" consultants.* The consulting firm promises to prepare specialized industry-specific recommendations to help improve a company's performance. The sales associates often promise the businesses will realize a very healthy ROI from their consulting services, and assure the business owners they'll easily be able to afford the consulting fees via the forthcoming increases in revenues and earnings.

After the small business owners agree to a consulting project the firm's consultants arrive, usually in pairs – each one bills the small business $275 per hour. In addition, the consulting firm charges the small businesses for the consultant's air fare, hotel, rental car, and per diem expenses. The consultants often produce reports and charts based on generic data and do not provide specialized recommendations for the small business client.

The consulting firm's sales associates are supposed to get commitments of at least 110 hours per consulting project to generate billings of $30,000 or more. Although the consultants who arrive on site are billed to the small business at $275 per hours, the contract labor consultants are only compensated at a rate of $35 per hour and are required to work from 7 a.m. to 10 p.m. to generate 15 billable hours per day – a daily cost of over $4,000 to the small business owner. It's no surprise the small businesses rarely realize any increase in profits. These small business are often left in a worse financial situation than before they entered into the agreement with the consulting firm. Although they paid a minimum of $30,000 in consulting fees, the small business owners receive no salient advice to optimize business operations or improve their company's revenue or profits.

The consulting firm's sales associates verbally promise the business owners they will not have to pay for consulting services if they are unsatisfied with the results. However, the consulting firm's written contracts make no such assurances and expressly state all terms of the agreement are defined within the contract. When small business owners complain about receiving unsatisfactory service and refuse to pay the balance due, the consulting firm is known for using aggressive collection practices to compel clients to pay per the terms of the written binding contract. Demands are put on the small business owners to make immediate payment. If the business owner refuses to pay the consultants are trained to remain on the premises until they receive a post-dated check from the business owner. When business owners refuse to make the final payment the consulting firm simply sues the small business for material breach of contract.

Is this consulting firm successful?

The company generates over $200 million in annual revenue and is extremely profitable. The consulting firm never provides references to prospective clients, never gets any repeat business, and is frequently the defendant in civil lawsuits. There have been hundreds of complaints about them filed with the Better Business Bureau and the State Attorney General's office.

How does this firm handle all the negative publicity and keep getting new clients? They change their company name and operate under several different "doing business as" names so they can establish plausible deniability when it comes to legitimate questions from would-be customers about their track record – stating their clients' confidential business practices and trade secrets as the reasons for the concealment. The firm assures potential clients their business matters will be treated with the same level of confidentiality.

This example is admittedly a very extreme case yet it illustrates the short-term focus of achieving immediate revenues, the total disregard for understanding customer needs, let alone any interest in providing value or retaining a customer. Churn 'em and burn 'em, indeed.

Understanding Market Dynamics

In contrast, companies that are genuinely market driven demonstrate an outlook that's much more long-term, and their approach concentrates on concepts like total customer satisfaction, managing the customer experience, customer retention, and customer lifetime value. Engaging customers at a level that enables a clear understanding of their needs presumes if customers are delighted, not only will the revenues come, but profits will escalate and growth will ensue.

Market driven companies are externally focused and gaze outside the company for the input required to develop solid strategies and make tactical decisions. Being market driven means developing a thorough understanding of market dynamics and consumer needs. This external focus makes opportunities more readily identifiable so the company can capitalize on them.

By staying connected to their customers and cultivating those important relationships, market driven companies are much better equipped than their sales driven rivals at anticipating market changes. Maintaining very close links to customers – and therefore to the market, the insight gained by companies that are market driven provides competitive advantages that greatly improve their ability to continually offer real value to customers.

Obsessing Over Consumer Needs

Well before the advent of the World Wide Web, my company, Datastorm Technologies was completely consumed with understanding the wants and needs of our customers and the fans of our data communication software, ProComm. As a market driven company, the entire organization was built around learning what customers found valuable and incorporating that information into features for each new product release. Datastorm utilized a flexible and powerful free-form database in both the technical support and customer service departments to store blurbs from conversations with customers regarding things they wished the product could do. With over 100 people in technical support collectively taking thousands of phone calls a day from consumers, vast amounts of data regarding requests for new features was captured, sorted, prioritized on a regular basis, and delivered to the system architects and project leaders in R&D. Datastorm had a sophisticated Voice of Customer program in place to help us thoroughly understand the wants and needs of consumers.

When calls came in from extremely experienced computer users who were operating within complex and sophisticated computing environments at large corporate, government or educational entities, those calls were escalated with priority and routed from technical support direct to a programmer in R&D who was very knowledgeable about that particular issue. Datastorm's programmers would engage these people and gain a thorough understanding of their computing environment so we could ascertain what would be required to adapt ProComm to meet the needs of organizations with similar situations.

Datastorm also had members of the technical support department attend computer user group meetings in large cities popular at the time. The technical support team member would give away a few free copies of ProComm, lots of cool ProComm T-shirts, and most importantly stand face-to-face with experienced computer users – listen to complaints about product quirks they didn't care for, and suggestions regarding everything from the user interface to features they'd like to see in the next product release.

Continually Soliciting Input From Customers

Members of Datastorm's field sales department were required to engage people with IT departments at the corporate, educational and government agencies that held enterprise-wide ProComm licenses. The goal was to gather as much information as possible about their opinions on emerging industry trends, and to solicit their feedback to learn what features these entities could utilize to make life easier within the IT department itself; and for the thousands of ProComm users within their organizations. Since this information was often over the heads of sales personnel, Datastorm had a key employee who was dedicated as the liaison between sales and R&D enabling this valuable information to be relayed to the department heads in R&D in the technological terms needed to put all this valuable data to good use.

In addition to our own corporate BBS, Datastorm maintained a ProComm Forum on CompuServe and GEnie, and engaged in dialogues with customers in these subscription-based online information services. Experienced and conversant ProComm fans were recognized and led or moderated round-table discussions, helping less knowledgeable ProComm users with technical issues or product tips. Brand advocates utilized their expertise for a myriad of different reasons – some love to help people while others craved recognition and wanted their proficiency to be well known. Regardless, the positive word of mouth generated by all these individuals was exceptionally valuable.

Naturally, Datastorm sent questionnaires and newsletters to ProComm users on a regular basis to request feedback on what they liked, didn't like, and what we could do to improve the product and their user experience. We also invited customers to share stories about interesting ways they were using our software in their organization, many of which were esoteric and fascinating.

Giving Customers Want They Want

ProComm's new feature sets, product enhancements and improvements enabled a more intuitive user interface were always based on exactly the specific items most requested from customers and passionate brand advocates. As a result, ProComm surpassed the competitive software program offerings from Microsoft and other Fortune 500 companies, and became the de facto standard in communications software, and is still the world's best-selling PC data communications software of all time. Datastorm experienced 40 consecutive profitable quarters of growth and ProComm became a global brand, published in 11 languages and they achieved over 70 percent market share in the product niche. Datastorm's 10 years of uninterrupted success was not a fluke – it was the outcome of being laser focused on our customers' wants and needs, and providing them with an extremely powerful program with an intuitive user interface – tremendous value at a very reasonable price. After Datastorm's acquisition; ProComm went on to become part of Symantec's product line and its success and popularity with computer users continued for several years.

Driving Datastorm's global achievements with ProComm was a wonderful time for me – our accomplishments were no accident. They were the result of continuously listening to customers, providing methods to engage them in communications, actively reminding them we genuinely valued their input, and would incorporate features designed to meet their needs into each new product release. Keeping such close ties to customers of all types – from the most novice to the most skilled, kept Datastorm very close to the market itself. This enabled us to anticipate market needs and continually offer a relevant software program that consumers valued and were genuinely passionate about.

Datastorm was a raw start-up company that boot-strapped with no outside funding whatsoever, and our customer-centric mindset was baked in from the very beginning. Developing an organization that's marketing driven isn't neuroscience, although it requires a great deal of commitment across the entire organization in order to be successful. Organizations that want to evolve and become adaptive must consciously make this a priority and dedicate enough attention so that it becomes the overarching strategic objective of their company. However company executives frequently miscalculate what is actually required to put such a dramatic change of business strategy into action. Companies get tripped up while attempting to implement market driven strategies because their organizations are poorly suited for such an undertaking.

Adapting to Become Market Driven

If your organization is not completely customer-centric, sweeping change isn't going to happen overnight. It's completely unrealistic to expect a sales driven or internally focused organization to suddenly have close ties to the market. It would be like taking the brass horn section from a philharmonic orchestra and expecting them to play the stringed instruments at next month's symphony just because they're virtuoso musicians. It simply isn't going to happen without reconditioning. Rethinking the whole organization and developing new competencies takes time. Executives talk about their companies becoming marketing driven, but having the wherewithal to effectively make such a comprehensive transformation throughout the organization is an altogether different story.

Successfully implementing and carrying out this strategy pivots on whether this mindset becomes a central part of a company's composition through and through — including the long-term allocation of sufficient capital and human resources, and an exceptional senior marketing executive. The senior-most marketers must be thought-leaders, more so than any other member of the executive team. The strategies they set quite literally mold the company's identity, drive business performance, and champion the customer's needs. Managers that operate at this level, shoulder great responsibility and need considerable latitude as their obligation to deliver is paramount.

With this realization it's apparent that CEOs along with marketing chiefs exert considerable influence in determining the direction of their corporation as one of the most vital decision makers in the organization. These challenges require the qualities of outstanding leaders and the support of CEOs who willingly embrace their marketing chiefs as strategic allies, and recognize that the wide-ranging issues which focus directly on customer satisfaction are the components most vital to ensuring the company's success. Chief executives who don't openly champion the endeavors of their senior marketer's efforts to be compulsive about continually delivering value to customers, do so at the peril of their organizations.

Chapter 5

ADAPTIVE MARKETING

Learning and Adjusting

Companies must become considerably more nimble and responsive. In this rapidly changing global marketplace relevance matters more than ever and is increasingly tied to what just happened recently. Brands must be contextual to consumers, and that means making significant changes away from contrived messages that are preached through the proverbial megaphone. Instead, marketers must provide relevant content crafted to resonate with consumers across multiple platforms. These activities must be monitored continuously so companies can learn how consumer sentiments are changing so organizations can adjust accordingly. Listening and monitoring enables marketing to ensure under-performing initiatives are curtailed, while the activities that show promise are enhanced and invested in more heavily.

This isn't easy, but it's what's required for success going forward. The ability to obtain insight and knowledge for making data-driven decisions based on real world information derived from constant monitoring is a huge departure from old familiar planning cycles. The CMO can't do this alone and must work in tandem with the CIO. It also requires the buy-in from the entire C-Suite and must be championed by the CEO.

Adaptive Marketing: Catalyst for Organizational Transformation

Rapid technological advances, transformations in media, and societal transitions have resulted in the metamorphosis of marketing into an adaptive period. Adaptive marketing is characterized by the considerable increases in one-to-one interplay between brands and consumers, and action designed specifically for individuals. The days of push marketing are waning fast giving way to strategies which zero in on the formation of experiences for individual consumers rather than campaigns aimed at target audiences. Those who are not in tune with how the proliferation of social media and the accompanying magnitude of digital new media has overtaken mass media, are already well behind the curve and must pick up the pace if they realistically hope to gain an understanding of what should be delivered in the way of marketing communications.

The ability for marketing on a one-to-one basis has been made possible by consumer's immersion in social media and marketer's ability to gain keen insight into consumers' sentiments and interact with them in real-time. It is vital for the intelligence gleaned about customers via research to be at the heart of all initiatives. To stay in harmony with their public, brands must go through the reinvention process continuously or face irrelevance. Maintaining this relevance is necessary to perpetually engage consumers; requiring expeditious adaptation and revisions in marketing strategies. CMOs and senior marketing executives must be empowered and have the capital and human resources necessary to tweak strategies and implement tactics.

These organizational transformations will prove challenging for many companies, especially large companies with multiple layers of management and a lot of bureaucracy – lumbering giants who can't get out of their own way are likely to struggle. Unless large companies can reorganize their hierarchical structures and ditch their decision by committee mentality for one that is entrepreneurial, they'll have a hard time taking courses of action at such a quickened pace.

Small companies who can turn on a dime and make decisions quickly may be able to seize the day and go from positions of being the market challengers to the market leaders in their niche. Marketing is rapidly becoming powered by technology; learning in near real-time has become crucial for identifying the company's direction and how to best position product and service offerings so they're more likely to be embraced by consumers.

Social Media as a Component Integrated Across the Enterprise

Forward-thinking enterprises are not merely limiting the deployment of social media to marketing efforts involving social networks, websites, blogs, PR, and search engine optimization; they are becoming adaptive organizations and realizing benefits from social media by utilizing it across their organization to obtain maximum impact in each department. Aside from marketing, the departments or functions within many organizations include R&D, Inside and Outside Sales; Business Development, Customer Service, Technical Support, Human Resources, Training, Information Technology, Accounting, Legal, Manufacturing, Operations, and Quality Control.

With your specific organization and its particular departments in mind, how can the implementation of social media assist each of these areas?

Organizational Obstructions to Adaptive Marketing

Pervasive social media across the enterprise requires change and let's face it, while change is one of the few constants in life, most people don't like change – at all. Many people are actually afraid of change.

Yet the key to developing a social media strategy requires getting buy-in from the C-Suite and across the organization. While there is absolutely no question social media marketing in particular is imperative, the number of senior executives who have their heels dug in and refuse to embrace social media is alarming.

When it comes to social media marketing, it's an understatement to say many organizations are not diving in head first. Internal barricades, trepidation, and apprehensions amongst other factors are keeping organizations from readily embracing social media.

Studies have indicated the primary reasons organizations are not adapting to utilizing social media marketing include a lack of internal resources, lack of time, executives aren't convinced there is value, lack of awareness, the belief that social media marketing is not appropriate for their company or brand, lack of clear policies, lack of guidelines for implementation, fear of negative reactions from customers, lack of reach, and lack of knowing how to find an appropriate agency partner.

Since you are reading this book, hopefully you don't feel uneasy about using social media. However, there's a good chance you may have to be the change agent within your organization and provide the rationale to help enlighten your management team and associates so they adapt and understand the ways of social media.

With your strategic social media marketing plan in place, what will you do to get your organization to support it? Who within your organization is like-minded and may be able to help you champion this cause for the benefit the organization overall?

Companies Are Taking a Wait and See Approach

Recent survey results regarding how social media marketing is perceived when it comes to budgeting are very telling. Seventeen percent have the perception social media is free and should be kept that way. Twenty-seven percent question why they should invest in social media because they feel the value is an unknown and participation in social media activities should be dealt with only as time permits. A full 49 percent of organizations consider social media to hold promise and will eventually produce ROI, and are making restrained increases in their budgets for social media marketing. A mere seven percent of organizations are increasing their social media marketing budgets munificently because their efforts have produced measurable ROI and warrant continual enhancement.

The 44 percent of these organizations who are doing next to nothing in the way of social media marketing are likely to find themselves in very precarious situations as time marches on and we approach the year 2020. Their short-sighted attitudes will keep them from being relevant during a time of tumultuous change. The 49 percent who are taking a wait and see attitude and proceeding with caution need to invest in social media and get on track while they still have time. The seven percent who have embraced social media marketing with gusto and are investing liberally to make continuous improvements are truly forward-thinking adaptive marketers who are positioning themselves to usurp the organizations with laissez-faire attitudes.

Business Intelligence and Customer Analytics

The myriad of business intelligence and near real-time analytical tools available for monitoring consumer sentiment enables perpetual measurements of the continual flow of content at a very granular level. Empowered with this valuable consumer intelligence, adaptive marketers have the insight to separate the wheat from the chaff and utilize the most pertinent data to quickly and accurately ascertain which content warrants reinvestment and which content shall be eliminated due to its under achievement. Adaptive marketing leads to an adaptive brand – one that adjusts its' course to stay on target.

The industry analysts and researchers at Gartner forecast that by 2017 companies' Chief Marketing Officers are likely to have larger IT budgets than the Chief Information Officer. Presently, marketing is already the buyer or influencer for 80 percent of certain marketing technologies; for digital marketing, mobile marketing, database marketing, e-commerce, marketing automation, content management systems, sales force automation, and customer analytics. The dawn of the Chief Marketing Technology Officer is now upon us.

Business intelligence must be at the center of adaptive marketing. Sophisticated social media monitoring software tools for real-time data collection and analysis which indicate consumer sentiment and provide insight are necessary to make informed decisions based on what was just learned. Developing an adroit approach to utilizing this data is imperative. Just because a company can measure everything doesn't mean they should. Utilizing a social media strategist to define a salient methodology that aligns with corporate objectives is often necessity to keep the company on track and fend off the "analysis paralysis" syndrome that typically coincides with having enormous volumes of data at hand.

That is not to say less is more when it comes to measurement. The goal is to facilitate knowledge-based decision making based on the discovery of market and consumer insights. Then to expeditiously disseminate the knowledge gained via those insights so it can be integrated throughout the organization to enhance innovation and develop competitive advantages that lead to growth, increases in revenue, and earnings.

Understanding What Consumers Value is Essential

The knowledge obtained via social media monitoring and listening platforms about consumer sentiment, what they like and don't like, what they want and don't want, and most importantly what consumers value, must be integrated throughout the organization because this information leads to a number of greater opportunities. As companies strive to become more market driven and adapt to this digital age, organizations must make adjustments so the entire business is positioned to benefit from the knowledge gleaned via insights that originated from marketing's social media monitoring and listening initiatives – without having to jump over hierarchal hurdles or cut through unnecessary red tape.

Adaptive marketing thought leaders are laying the necessary underpinnings by actively utilizing social media analytics and other forms of business intelligence to make germane decisions that allow ongoing engagements and interactions with consumers. Recognizing and enabling the most impassioned loyal consumers as brand ambassadors and advocates literally builds brand. Forward-thinking companies will forgo the internal turf wars and corporate politics to leverage the important information that originated in marketing. The insights gained from consumers will influence vital matters like direct access from customer feedback to R&D, concepts for an innovative service offering, enhanced product development processes, critical time to market issues, the "sweet spot" for price points, competitors' activities, avoiding a potential crisis, managing a crisis that just transpired, improved customer service, and reduced customer service costs.

With organizations' new emphasis on real-time monitoring and listening, and ongoing measurement of consumer sentiments and values, organizations need not look at errors as failures, but as learning opportunities – opportunities that enable real, newfound knowledge which should be implemented immediately. Adopting a continuous learning cycle results in making adjustments to an offering while it's still in development rather than waiting until it's completely finished. If the company missed the mark a lot of money has already been spent; yet the market may have moved on reducing that offering's relevance. After an arrow has been shot from a bow the trajectory of the arrow can't be adjusted while it's still in flight. But if the arrow's path could be corrected while in flight to ensure it strikes much closer to the bull's eye, that would be another story! Several months of theoretical testing in a controlled environment doesn't ensure consumers will embrace a product. Although listening and learning to obtain ongoing feedback during the development stage greatly enhances the likelihood of an offerings' success in the marketplace with less risk and less expense in the long run.

Content Must Be Relevant

It is estimated that Americans are inundated with approximately 2,000 brand impressions daily – more than the great grandparents of the oldest Baby Boomers were exposed to during their entire lifetimes. We now live in an attention-based economy where people's attention is an increasingly scarce commodity. As a result consumers demand information that's authentic and completely relevant to them and their current life situation. They have less tolerance for irrelevance and want content that's both relevant and timely. If the information consumers are receiving is not perceived as authentic or relevant, they just move on mentally. There are simply too many other choices.

On any given day, the media alternative consumers have to choose from includes over 200 cable television networks, 5,500 magazine titles, and more than 2.5 billion websites. Having such a vast myriad of media choices and being well in control of their media world, consumers have less trouble finding content that's relevant to them. As marketers are beginning to accept that consumers are in control, they must develop expertise with the various social platforms utilized by consumers and increase their understanding of how consumers use them. Then, marketers can contour their content and marketing campaigns so they reach consumers with more surgical precision and deliver relevant messages that have impact.

Communications Should be Interwoven Across Platforms

Americans have now made obvious how their attraction to the Internet, affinity to social networks, and their proclivity for rapidly moving across multiple platforms functions as a mechanism for completely new types of communication. Clearly marketers should target consumers using methods that are increasingly interwoven so that the content and messaging in one communications platform interplays in a distinctly different form that's more pertinent to other media platforms.

Just as additional content has been made available on Director's Cut or Special Edition DVDs for years, marketers can extend the appeal of their brands to consumers by making additional content available on the company's website and across all aspects of their social media network. Companies must work to enhance the significance of their existing platforms by embracing burgeoning technologies and by implementing creative strategies. Streaming online video, text messaging, online games, smartphones, mobile devices, and one-to-one relationships enabled by social networks should all be considered as platforms that can be effectively utilized to reach consumers.

Social Media as a Component of the Integrated Marketing Strategy

Social media marketing is not a silo and must not be treated as such. It has become a vital component of the overall strategic marketing mix. Marketing strategies and the accompanying tactics should be fully integrated in the first place. Social media marketing is no exception. Adaptive marketers are wisely moving it to the hub of all their marketing initiatives.

The integration of the social media marketing components into the existing marketing mix isn't particularly difficult. What's more the integration of social media marketing will demonstrate its value as the whole of social media marketing (combined with other marketing tactics) creates results notably greater than the sum of its parts.

Chapter 6

DEVELOPING A SOCIAL MEDIA MARKETING STRATEGY

Why Bother Developing a Strategy?

Organizations need to create a plan for the strategic use of social media just like they need to develop a business plan. The document that results from developing a strategy serves as a guide for the organization's methodology for utilizing social media for the needs of the business and its' customers, both now and in the future. A company without a documented strategy for their social media initiatives is like a schooner without a destination or a rudder. Without charts or a rudder, strong gusts of wind that fill the sails are of no benefit to the vessel.

Creating a Social Media Marketing Strategy is Absolutely Essential

Social media marketing is not a magic elixir. It's an increasingly important and very necessary component of the marketing mix. And like other components in the marketing mix, strategies must come before tactics. Few things can live up to the hype surrounding social media. The term itself has become a misnomer because it's incorrectly used as a catch all term for so many things – which adds to misconceptions for those who are new to implementing social media marketing. When it comes to creating a social media marketing strategy companies must get their head around a simple concept. The

47

objective is not to excel at social media per se. The objective is to effectively utilize social media to help your business excel. Over thinking social media initiatives often makes creating social media marketing strategies more difficult than necessary.

Don't Make It Difficult

Companies frequently struggle with developing a social media strategic plan; the process becomes arduous and the plan is muddled.

From my experience the problem pertains to how conflicted organizations are about social media overall. For many it's new and different – that brings about uncertainty. Companies know they need to be innovative but don't want to crash and burn in the process. Many of them want to adopt a fresh approach, but they worry about the accompanying risk. They want to act swiftly and be adaptable, but don't want to give up control. They hear that successful social media marketing requires empowering a number of people cross-departmentally, yet they want to hold on to the decision making process for themselves. They are uncomfortable with experimentation – preferring when things are more conventional. They understand input from customers has value, but they don't want efficiency to wane.

It's challenging for organizations to transform from their existing state to one that's considerably more nimble. And the idea of becoming a learning organization comes with the inherent admission that they don't know everything. But that's OK – as an applied science, marketing has undergone tremendous change in recent years – and the changes will continue. Knowing change is coming causes some to feel vulnerable but no organization is alone – these changes affect everyone – and organizations around the world are all learning at their own pace.

While posting tweets about strategy and innovation on Twitter, I often use the hashtag, #FailFaster. Experimentation will result in some failures along the way. From mistakes that come from doing things differently there will be newfound knowledge to apply to improve processes, innovation, and the creation of value for customers. Clearly, social media initiatives require completely letting go of the status quo, which is easier said than done but essential for success.

Learn From Others' Mistakes

Before we really get into social media strategy there are some lessons to be learned from mistakes made by the vast majority of companies – putting tactics before the strategies.

Frankly this is an area where I see many organizations really stumble. After finally deciding to establish a social media presence the company wants to move quickly and has a check-list mentality. My observation of this way of thinking equates to the disbelief that the social marketing initiatives will provide any real value – yet everyone seems to be doing it so let's get this over with so we can check it off our "to do" list and get back to business. And so it goes. The company has an online presence set up on the most popular social media networks without consideration to strategy.

In their haste, with no regard for strategies, goals or overall objectives, their social marketing efforts are incongruent with the organization's raison d'être. The results of their desultory efforts are lackluster at best. Poor results reinforce the popular preconceived misconception held by a vast percentage of executives that social media marketing does not work and has no value – which is clearly not true.

Because social media is still a new area to many companies' their dearth of knowledge about it is to be expected. Besides the obvious half-hearted stab at establishing a social presence here's a major underlying problem: Companies are not properly investing in sufficient education and training regarding the ways of social media, especially in social media strategy. The lack of knowledge is understandable. However pressing on without a basic understanding, let alone any real know-how or expertise is reckless. On average, American corporations spend a mere $25,000 obtaining knowledge to better understand social media – so it's not surprising why ill-prepared companies make poor decisions in their social endeavors.

Learn From Others' Success

Some of the companies having great success with their social media initiatives come from the sectors that were early adopters to social media. Those sectors are media, telecommunications and technology. Approximately 25% of the companies in these sectors claim their social media marketing was steadily integrated into their companies' processes as social media networks emerged. Organizations in other sectors like the healthcare and financial services industries are ramping up their knowledge of the aspects integrating social media into their enterprises due to legal, compliance, and privacy issues. Companies in regulated industries that see the benefits of social media have little choice but to invest in obtaining all the knowledge required to stay within the law. They're likely to have great success with their social media marketing initiatives as a result of the education they acquired about social media in the process of learning about legal compliance.

Align Social Media Marketing With Your Organization's Business Strategies and Objectives

If you feel apprehensive about developing a social media strategy take a few hours and ignore you're working on a strategy for social media. Think of it as strategies for your business – because that's what it is. The owners of small businesses, executives at Fortune 500 companies, and managers at companies of every size in between should be accustomed to developing strategies for their organization. If not, I strongly suggest you immediately do a deep dive into strategy, immerse yourself and get up to speed quickly. A college course on business strategy would be very helpful. You may want to read some of the writings by the "business thinker" – the late, great Peter Drucker, or by Harvard Business School professor, Michael E. Porter. (Note: Michael Porter's course, The Microeconomics of Competitiveness and Corporate Strategy was the toughest, most intellectually stimulating and gratifying class I took while earning my MBA). If your company does not have defined business strategies, you're really not ready to implement anything in the way of social media. Please feel free to contact me if you'd like help developing your strategies.

Strategies define sets of processes that need to be implemented to achieve goals. Effective strategies require vision and a thorough understanding of your business' purposes and values. Vision keeps the enterprise moving while values keep it stable. Strategies need not be complicated. Quite simply the organization is presently here at Point A, and it wants to get there to Point B, and it wants this progress to occur in a certain amount of time. Management outlines goals and objectives that will move them from where they are to where they want to be by the end of the next quarter, by the fiscal year end, in three years from now – whatever the timeframe may be. The goals and objectives are as varied as the types of companies that exist. The leaders of the organization should know what will be required to move their business forward, define what those things are, and make them known throughout the enterprise so they can be understood and supported – so they can be achieved. Aligning social media marketing with the organization's strategy draws a distinct connection between business goals and the processes necessary to achieve those goals.

Define Your Organization's Marketing Strategies and Objectives

The development of a business-aligned social media marketing strategy development needs to start with the identification of organizational goals – the goals that propel the organization's planning and operational endeavors.

Indentifying online and offline marketing goals entails working with senior marketing management to select the three to five main marketing goals, and to decide on which corresponding metrics the organization will utilize to determine whether or not the organization successfully achieves the goals. Many companies do not measure how their social media marketing efforts shore up nor augment their traditional and digital marketing strategies – this is a mistake.

It's very important to get agreement from senior marketing management on these goals at the beginning of this strategy project since these goals will set the priorities of prospective actions that will be implemented in the social media initiatives.

Formal organizations are likely to already have corporate goals in place and incorporated into long-term planning and budgeting processes. Other organizations may require assistance defining a cohesive set of goals. Regardless, it's essential to comprehend and clearly communicate what the organization is attempting to accomplish.

Define Your Organization's Marketing Functions

With your organization's marketing goals identified you're ready to define the marketing functions performed by various groups within the organization. That is, the activities directly tied to supporting the defined objectives.

In large organizations the process of defining the many various marketing functions that explain the work performed within the organization may not directly link to a formal hierarchical structure – due to the existing overlap of responsibilities across departments.

Examples of Social Media Marketing Goals and Objectives

With your organization's strategies, overall goals, objectives, and organizational functions clearly defined, but prior to making definitive decisions on setting social media priorities and choosing the appropriate channels for the various initiatives, the social media goals need to be aligned with organizational goals. Forming a list to characterize the specific social media marketing goals is a must.

The first item on the list needs to be listening, via a robust social media monitoring / listening platform. The next chapter of this book discusses listening in detail.

Below are examples for your list:

- Generate more leads
- Increase brand awareness
- Understand what consumers are saying about your brand
- Promote an event
- Obtain more coverage in the press
- Get feedback on the quality of your customer service
- Triple the number of people in your e-mail list

- Establish your CEO as a thought leader in your industry niche
- Identify brand advocates and fans
- Raise awareness about a particular cause
- Request donations for a charitable organization
- Drive more traffic to a particular page on your website
- Recruit new members
- Influence public opinion about a specific issue
- Solicit photos / videos taken at a fund-raising event
- Provide a glimpse of what goes on "behind the scenes"
- Disseminate information about a new offering
- Double the amount of foot traffic to retail outlets
- Shift sales to your e-commerce site
- Stay informed on competitors' maneuvers
- Reach more of the Millennial audience
- Create a public forum where advocates can show support
- Enroll volunteers

I could go on and on but these are some examples to get you rocking and rolling.

Prioritize and Define Social Media Marketing Objectives

After creating a list leave listening at the top; carefully prioritize your list with the chief objectives, (aside from listening) in descending order. While in line with organizational goals these objectives must be unambiguous, pragmatic, achievable, and have a definite time frame attached to each of them.

Note: Aside from listening and monitoring (which are paramount and should be continuous) starting with just three to five key objectives is important to keep the social media marketing initiatives manageable so they can be well-executed. The sheer volume of data that is returned via social media monitoring and listening is immense and can seem daunting; like drinking water from a fire hose. This data must be vetted and transformed into information that is useful and actionable. The attempt to tackle every organizational objective simultaneously is completely unrealistic and will result in ineffectual campaigns with poor results. The notion that effective social media marketing is easy is a myth!

Clearly explain in writing how each of the social media objectives specifically assists or is directly connected to defined goals.

Define Specific Social Media Marketing Initiatives

With the objectives defined and prioritized, and a "short list" in place, the specific initiatives must be defined. Below are examples of specific initiatives:

- Create and maintain a presence on Facebook for purposes of corporate marketing and identifying loyal customers.
- Create Twitter accounts for the experts within the company to tweet on specific topics related to the market niche, and to interact with existing and potential customers on a one-to-one basis.
- Create a blog for the CEO to establish him or her as a thought leader in the industry.
- Write an informative eBook about best practices in your industry niche; post it on the company's web site so it is available for anyone who provides their e-mail address to download as a PDF file.
- Organize "Hangouts" on Google+ where loyal customers and brand advocates can engage the company and each other in live video chats.

Defining Success

Following the identification of the top objectives and writing descriptions about how they align with organizational goals, the next step is to ascertain how you will characterize small victories during social media marketing campaigns.

Victories may be characterized as:

- The number of people following your organization on LinkedIn
- The number of retweets on Twitter
- The number of new leads for the sales team
- The amount of earned media coverage received
- Increase in the number of new visitors to your website
- Increase in the number of page views on your website
- Increase in the average amount of time spent on your website
- Increase in comments to blog posts
- Increase in revenue via e-commerce site
- Increase in downloads of an informative White Paper
- Increase in the number of views of your video on YouTube
- Increase in the number of "Likes" of your video on YouTube
- Decrease in number of calls into the Customer Care Department
- Decrease in the duration of calls handled by Customer Care
- Identification of individuals who are brand advocates
- Innovative product development ideas that come from customers

Again these are examples. Your organizations' small victories will be coupled to your objectives and specific social media marketing initiatives via the metrics you identify. The organization needs a performance framework that links social media marketing efforts to business Key Performance Indicators (KPIs) across the enterprise. Metrics will be covered in Chapter 9.

Allocate All the Necessary Resources to Ensure Success

Even with business, marketing, social media strategies well defined, and a clear understanding of social media objectives and tactics in place, adequate human and financial resources must be allocated to social media marketing initiatives. Great plans are important – great execution to carry out those plans is equally important. Executing social media initiatives requires ongoing efforts – with those efforts there are expenses. Doing social media marketing well requires a significant amount of time, trained personnel and the overhead costs associated with the human resources. While there are no fees charged by social media networks to establish a presence on their platforms, social media initiatives are not free. There are costs associated with investing in the necessary monitoring / listening software tools to observe consumers' behavior and sentiment as it pertains to your social networks and social web. There are also costs associated with offerings to engage them in dialogues as well as costs involved with attempting to move them from members of the general public to eventually becoming paying customers.

Whether these initiatives are done within the company, or in conjunction with experienced consultants like me, there will be costs involved with expanding these efforts. Regardless, the proper strategies must be in place first, and proceeding without them is nothing short of careless. There are certainly opportunity costs associated with not proceeding with social media marketing, as well as with proceeding haphazardly and going about it all wrong. The importance of strategy can't be stressed enough!

Chapter 7

PERSISTENT LISTENING

Ongoing Listening is at the Heart of Every Successful Social Media Strategy

It's a vital component.

Listening to learn is where a company typically begins. For instance, learning the company's Share of Voice compared to that of their competitors is something marketers can determine relatively quickly. During the early stages of listening companies tend to react to what they've learned. Over time, full-on continuous social listening enables meaningful intelligence to permeate the enterprise and extend to the individuals within the organization who are best suited to comprehend the information – and act on it accordingly. The sooner a company can get to the point where their persistent listening is proactive the better. Proactive listening is part of "purposeful listening" based on business objectives and metrics to support KPIs.

Obtaining Meaningful Intelligence

Obtaining meaningful intelligence from advanced monitoring and listening toolsets necessitates human brainpower to make decisions on the multiple fine distinctions required for comprehension and action. While advanced technologies are a must for meaningful intelligence, human interaction is essential to grasp the clear gist of conversations, as well as the equivocal undertones – the nuances of which are misunderstood or undetected by even the most advanced technological toolsets. In spite of their sophisticated linguistic algorithms, limitations are inherent to the most professional grade listening platforms, and are able to accurately identify sentiment about 60 percent of the time. This is due to the continual and rapid evolution of human language. Google asserts 20 percent of queries made each month were never searched previously. Not surprising when you know the Urban Dictionary is appended with several hundred new words every day! Slang, jargon, cynicism and implied sentiment make correctly indentifying sentiment extremely difficult for machine intelligence. Considering the sheer magnitude of data being scraped, collected and sifted, 60 percent accuracy is impressive. However, people performing analysis must be combined with advanced technologies to ensure scalability, accuracy and integrity of discoveries.

Understanding Consumer Sentiment

On a standalone basis, even the most advanced listening tools pale at determining sentiment compared to human beings. For instance, on its own, a listening platform doesn't know what to make of a statements like, "My new Android device rocks ;^)" or "The band at The Roxy Theatre on Sunset Blvd. killed last night!" In my personal experience working on strategic social media marketing initiatives, I've seen the best in class listening platform incorrectly score statements from the social web like these examples above. Without human guidance, machine intelligence would label, "My new Android device rocks ;^)" as a statement with neutral sentiment because it doesn't understand the very positive connotation associated with the word "rocks" – or the smiling emoticon at the end of the statement. Similarly, machine intelligence would label, "The band at The Roxy Theatre on Sunset Blvd. killed last night!" with negative sentiment because it doesn't understand the word "killed" used in the vernacular is highly complementary of the band at the famous rock and roll venue in Hollywood.

These two examples are for illustration purposes and the majority of people familiar with today's lexicon of colloquial language and slang words could correct the sentiment scores on each of the statements above as positive. However, while working on projects for companies with highly technical offerings, it was necessary for me to become very familiar with the technological aspects of the offerings to properly adjust the sentiment score initially labeled by the listening software tools. The real world cases of scoring sentiment properly aren't nearly as overt as the ones I used in the examples above. Thorough understandings of the organization, their goals and objectives, products and services are required, as well as focused concentration on heaps of data.

In addition, a person can discover unexpected gems of information they came across and know are valuable that the algorithms in the listening tools were not specifically seeking in the data. Experienced people analyzing the listening tools' findings are able to discover nuggets of knowledge they deem relevant to the brand, to the conversation, to an internal process, to the R&D team, to the CFO, to the compliance or legal department. These types of discoveries are made via human intelligence and intuition while sifting through findings from advanced listening tools – gut instincts and inklings are skill sets algorithms lack.

Knocking Down Silos

Valuable analytical data must not remain in a silo. Information gleaned from social media monitoring and listening needs to be combined with web analytics and customer data from CRM to enable knowledge-based decisions for the enterprise. Persistent purposeful listening puts the concentration on organization's business objectives.

With specific company goals in focus, proactive monitoring and listening will help pinpoint the essential KPIs that will indicate when those goals have been achieved. Best practices include configuring specific listening solutions and defining the social metrics that reasonably support the KPIs.

Increasingly sophisticated understanding and use of analytics sheds light on how to configure listening solutions so meaningful intelligence and insights are available for R&D and product managers, and to measure specific marketing campaigns and adjust them in near real-time. Over time, more complex listening practices may be implemented across the enterprise, as the meaningful intelligence provides insight on how to streamline operations and knock down silos for greatly improved cross-departmental workflow and more efficient collaboration throughout the enterprise. Executives need to enthusiastically champion this cause and be readily willing to revamp business processes based on what is learned from relevant insights. Enterprises must be nimble so meaningful intelligence can permeate the organization and reach the teams or team member best-suited to expeditiously act upon the information.

This is an example of how adaptive marketing evolves into making the whole organization adaptive. The benefits that result from this necessary evolution helps move the enterprise away from the dreaded status quo.

Walking Before You Run

Focusing on important activities crucial to the organization's success – and can be measured – proves challenging. I strongly suggest selecting a small number of different projects to pilot during the learning process. Until some semblance of proficiency is achieved, trying to run with a large number of requirements usually leads to frustration and no progress to speak of. After the KPIs have been determined, listening should be arranged around the specific objectives, which involves tailoring metrics specific to the brand, company, Voice of Customer, products, Share of Voice, competitors, competitive products, and so on. These initial configurations are required to reveal the meaningful intelligence from persistent social listening.

Share of Conversation

In days gone by brands placed a lot of emphasis on their Share of Voice – the brand's advertising weight expressed as a percentage of a defined total market or market segment during a specific period of time. Share of Voice visually depicts increases or decreases in advertising weight compared to brands' competitors. A graphic representation of how your brand's advertising ranked amongst the competition during a given month was nice to have, but has less pertinence today, as it doesn't portray what really matters now – what consumers are talking about, and their sentiments. Consumers don't spend time thinking about how much advertising one company is spending to promote their brand compared to a competitive brand. Consumers think about what's important to them.

Social media has changed the world forever, and the ability to understand your brand's Share of Conversation across the social web is extremely important. The messaging created and disseminated by brands via advertisements and press releases has only a fraction of the impact of what's being said via conversations and product reviews relevant to your brand that are posted online by consumers. Social media monitoring shows how Share of Conversation is multitudes greater in volume than Share of Voice, and equally greater in relevance to brands.

Example: Using Social Media Monitoring to Understand Share of Conversation

Here's a revealing example from a recent engagement I had with a publicly-traded software company based in California.

In the months prior to me being contacted by the corporation's Chief Marketing Officer, the company released a handful of utility software programs that competed directly with the leading products in three separate vertical market niches. As the market challenger in each of these niches, the software company's intent was to lure customers away from the market leaders in these immature market niches that showed promising growth. Two quarters after the launch of the challenger software programs, the revenue generated by these products were dismal at best. The company's CMO needed a better understanding of what adjustments needed to be made with their marketing efforts, and where to allocate resources accordingly.

I utilized the powerful web-based social media research platform offered by Spiral16 for listening to, measuring, and visualizing the Share of Conversation for the company's software programs, the competitive software programs, and the market niches.

Within two weeks I presented the company's CMO with the detailed results from the listening initiative. Based on what I knew when I started the project, I was not surprised by the findings. And while the CMO was disheartened, the results confirmed his gut feeling that the challenger products his company had launched were receiving almost no Share of Conversation whatsoever. On separate pie charts, each of these products Share of Conversation looked like tiny slivers representing less than two percent of the pie. The overwhelming majority of the talk, positive Word of Mouth, recommendations, and online reviews posted by consumers were about the software products that had already reached the market leader positions in their respective nascent niches.

The real-world information gleaned provided the CMO with the necessary data required to make informed decisions. Revenue from these products was not going to contribute to the company's quarterly targets during the last half of their fiscal year, the company was going to fall short of stock market analysts' estimates, and their share price was going to take a significant hit. At the same time, there was absolutely no reason to spend additional millions of dollars in advertising and promotion. This was a classic case of the Law of Diminishing returns. The prudent thing to do was make a strategic retreat and withdraw these software products from their respective market niches. Accepting defeat never feels good. However, making business decisions based on emotions isn't fiduciarily responsible. Emotional maturity is required to make decisions that are in the best interest of the organization.

In spite of all the hype, social media for business is still in its early stages. And while it's not new overall, it is new to businesses all over the world, so naturally the innovative tools that should be used in conjunction with social media aren't on the radar screens of these companies. As businesses become more aware of the powerful insights available from listening tools and social media monitoring, they won't be using them in a reactionary mode like in the real world example above. They'll be using them as advanced social media research tools that give companies the insight they need to make smarter decisions and gain competitive advantages.

The Ideal Approach

Here's what the California-based software company could have done instead, had they been aware of social media monitoring tools a year earlier.

Rather than spending significant amounts of time and money for R&D to develop these programs, and millions of dollars in the launch to bring them to market and promote them, the company could have spent a miniscule fraction of that money listening to learn about consumers' sentiments. The company would have seen how much momentum, loyalty, and market share the competitive software products that were first to market had already achieved. From that knowledge, the CMO would have known there was no way this handful of products could compete in the hot, new market categories, unless each one had at least one substantial differentiator in the way of enhanced feature sets, convenience, ease of use; or pricing. This knowledge would have made it clear that "me too" products that offered no additional value or benefits above and beyond the market leaders' software programs would surely fail. With a little more time and a little more money spent on listening to conversations about the competitive software products, the company could have determined the source of dissatisfaction regarding one of those products. Then, they could have dedicated their R&D team to creating a much more robust challenger software product to compete head on with the competitive program, and possibly usurped it to become the market leader in that niche.

Voice of Customer

Achieving proficiency with monitoring and listening benefits the entire organization. Until such time, the initial components of persistent listening typically best served the marketing department by providing the ability to identify exceptionally valuable brand advocates; and the customer service department by enabling them to provide better care across the multiple social platforms where companies' customers are sharing their opinions. As organizations become more adept with their listening capabilities, they should be able to leverage their increased competence to benefit the enterprise as a whole. Some of the most important benefits are improved customer retention and increased customer loyalty. Companies with the lowest customer churn rates and highest levels of new business via referrals are the companies that provide the best customer experiences. The ability to provide the best possible customer experiences requires a deep understanding of what customers' want, like, and value; the Voice of the Customer needs to be heard loud and clear.

Companies have a myriad of different product and service offerings, and define their customers' experiences according to those offerings. Businesses that have yet to define their customers' experiences need to create a definition by contemplating how their customers perceive specific interactions with the company, the company's employees, business processes, products or services, and how customers feel collectively about all those interactions.

Customers Remain Loyal to Companies That Provide Great Experiences

Customers are significantly more reluctant to take their business away from companies that provide them with the best customer experiences. In addition, customers are more likely to recommend companies that provide the best customer experiences. Savvy, adaptive companies understand that providing customers with a great experience is a key source of differentiation. Word of mouth is driven by customer's experiences and news travels fast – bad news travels faster. Surveys indicate customers are three times more likely to tell family, friends, and colleagues about deficient customer experiences than about first-rate experiences. This phenomenon illustrates the consequences of lackluster customer experiences – they push customers away, and hinder the ability to obtain new ones.

Prior to a company improving customer experiences they must understand where their current offerings fall short of meeting expectations. Multiple platforms and various customer touch points across those platforms make this more difficult than one might think. Since a company can't enrich what they don't understand, incorporating Voice of Customer is vital to improving customer experiences.

For instance, organizations implement processes designed to support interactions with customers, and these processes are part of customers' real-world experiences. However, how does an organization know how those processes impact customer experiences? The processes were put in place for a reason, but only the Voice of Customer affords the ability to understand if the processes unintentionally put barriers to purchase in place, cause customers to become confused, or make doing business with a company more arduous.

Since only a fraction of unhappy customers will actually complain to a company about their experience, the company is unaware of the meager experience, while the customer is spreading the information to their family, friends, and peer groups. Persistent listening enables individual customers to be identified and dialogues to ensue. When the Voice of Customer is being heard in the company, the company knows what went wrong and has the opportunity to remedy a customer's poor experience by acting quickly to make things right.

Nordstrom's Provides Excellent Customer Service

A few months ago I was on Twitter looking at my account settings. During that short time, I noticed someone had just followed me, so I clicked on their profile to see if it was someone I wanted to follow back. It was a 26 year old lady in Austin, Texas who I'll refer to by her middle name, Marie. During the minute it took to scan her bio and glance at her last few tweets, I noticed she had just tweeted 15 minutes before about how she felt flustered by a salesperson at Nordstrom's while shopping for a gift and left the store without buying anything. I didn't think much of it, and clicked the button to follow her back. During that very moment, a social media customer service representative from Nordstrom's sent a tweet to Marie, apologized for her unpleasant experience and asked for the store location where she'd been shopping.

This really piqued my interest!

Nordstrom's is renowned for their exceptional customer service, and the personnel in their stores are known for going to great lengths to ensure their clientele has great customer experiences. Nordstrom's empowers their employees to go to these lengths on the sales floor, and I was curious to see how the famous Nordstrom's customer service would translate to a social network platform. There are a lot of demands on my time, but since this was a textbook case of best practices by Nordstrom's, I decided to stay on Marie's Twitter page for a few minutes to see if she would reply.

Sure enough, within a few minutes Marie replied to Nordstrom's Twitter account and stated she was at the Barton Creek Store in Austin looking for a gift for a friend. At that point, the representative from Nordstrom's suggested that Marie continue via direct messages on Twitter to explain the situation so she could understand the problem and work to resolve the situation. This was classic! Through their social media listening efforts, Nordstrom's was able to rapidly respond to a lady who had an unpleasant experience in one of their stores, and then engage her in a real-time dialogue in an effort to remedy the situation that caused Marie to feel flustered and leave the store in Austin without making a purchase.

I contacted Nordstrom's and told them about what I witnessed firsthand and congratulated them on their use of best practices of customer service on social networks! I also contacted Marie to find out the rest of the story, and learned what happened when the "public" conversation on Twitter went offline to direct messages. Marie was delighted to share. She even e-mailed me screen shots from her computer monitor of the actual direct messages between her and Nordstrom's so I could see what transpired. Upon reading the direct messages Marie sent me, I saw Nordstrom's social media customer representative escalated her case to a gentleman who made arrangements to send her a gift card.

Actual Customer Interactions Increases Employee Empathy

Listening to understand Voice of Customer enables the employees at companies to be keenly aware of the interactions customers have had with those companies. This brings about an interesting phenomenon where employees turn out to be much more empathetic from hearing actual feedback that's directly attributed to a real customer's actual interaction. This level of context results in much deeper involvement with customers by the employees. The faster a company can engage a customer regarding a specific interaction the better. In the case above with Marie, Nordstrom's wasn't able to engage her at the store because Marie left in frustration and the company had no knowledge of Marie's specific interaction. However, when Marie made her interaction known via Twitter, Nordstrom's responded with urgency. And they responded via the same social media platform Marie utilized. Rapid response enables companies to obtain details regarding a specific customer interaction while it's still very fresh in their mind, which allows the company to acquire accurate data so decisions are based on reliable information.

Understanding Voice of Customers Provides Long-Term Value

Maintaining ongoing dialogues with customers allows insight into what the company is accomplishing. Voice of Customer is not a snapshot from one certain moment. It must be considered a conversation that provides long-term value, and enables companies to see what resonates with customers, and what isn't working and needs improvement. This requires the data acquired from specific customer interactions to be shared across the enterprise in a timely fashion. The longer specific information regarding customer interactions remains in a silo, the more the value of the information diminishes. Data that exists in a vacuum fundamentally constrains the ability to understand how customers feel. Research indicates most organizations fail to appreciate how comprehensive and widespread their Voice of Customer initiatives should be, and don't recognize the need for the flow of data across departments. In addition to the actual point of purchase, processes in various departments have a bearing on customers' experiences, which is why timely sharing of information is important – insight enables proper identification of the departments that need to make improvements, and details from specific interactions help departments discover where and how to improve.

SOCIAL MEDIA MONITORING CASE STUDIES - Courtesy of Spiral16

Case 1 – Why Medical and Healthcare Companies Need Online Monitoring

Online monitoring is becoming an integral component of medical and healthcare marketing. More healthcare companies are using online monitoring for their businesses because more consumers are using online health information to obtain second opinions, as well as a means by which to explore alternative treatments.

There is no big mystery as to why the web has become an invaluable resource to people looking for health-related information. We often feel helpless as it relates to our own care and well-being, and searching online allows people to feel more in control of their health and life situations.

While social networks play an important part in health seekers' online life, the vast majority begin their searches for information via a traditional search engine like Google; not via social networks. This means any listening strategy needs to be built around solutions that provide context beyond just social platforms to help understand how health facilities, providers, or communities appear online.

Online monitoring and listening by healthcare companies can inform strategy as well as more efficiently direct resources to their audience. The underlying research shows why online monitoring is extremely valuable for companies in the healthcare sector, and shows the statistics behind the growing consumer demand.

A recent study from the Pew Internet and American Life Project called these information seeking consumers "Health Seekers." More than half of the Health Seekers conducting online searches for medical information were searching for someone else. Over 72 percent of Health Seekers were looking for information about a specific illness or condition. This makes perfect sense as the children of the Baby Boomers grow older and are concerned about healthcare for their parents.

Reasons why people go online for healthcare resources:

- Tentatively diagnosing their own condition
- Confirming their doctor's diagnosis and suggested treatments
- Checking their doctors' credentials
- Researching all available treatment options – not just those recommended by their doctor
- Researching specific medical conditions when they (or a loved one) are diagnosed
- Connecting with other patients with the same disease
- Exploring and signing up for clinical trials

For healthcare companies, understanding what information their customers may find out about their organization is as important as what your potential customers are saying about your company or brand. Monitoring helps focus business priorities – saving valuable time and resources.

Brand management is one of the most popular applications for social media and web monitoring, but it isn't the only way to use a business intelligence platform. It's important to realize that companies can look at all kinds of online data sets to solve problems for their business. Here's another example of how companies use social media monitoring.

Case 2 – Automotive Group Identifies Market Trends and Web Influencers

The Client

A successful automotive retailer owns a number of new and used car dealerships across the Midwest. The parent company embraced the interactivity of social media by launching a blog that asked prospective car buyers how they feel the dealership experience can be improved.

The Challenge

The company discovered one local website to partner with for promotions, but the sample size relating to some of the specific new car information in strictly local markets is unstable. For this reason, the company monitors national trends and applies this data to their dealerships in local markets.

How They Utilized Social Media Monitoring

The company monitors national consumer trends in car sales and to track what consumers are talking about relating to new car issues. Over the previous year, the primary focus had been listening to what consumers were saying about Nissan cars. In addition to monitoring national trends, the company conducts comparative research on other industry leaders in automotive sales to obtain benchmarks for successful advertising and social media promotions.

Results from Six Months of Monitoring

- Identified online forums and blogs where people talk about the Nissan brand and buying cars.
- The company knows where to become a part of the discussion and where to engage the community to establish their position as authoritative figures in the online space.
- By identifying trends in other markets, the company adapted successful promotions for their dealership.
- The company's brand icon from their blog site uses data to find trends in car buying and car news to provide a competitive edge in content development.

- In blogs and social media mentions, the company discovered that reviews make up a large percentage of these results.

Why This Matters to Your Business

Social media and web monitoring is not just for big businesses or high-tech companies – it can be adapted to find all kinds of information. In addition to general brand management and learning what regional customers are saying, the automotive company uses social media monitoring to discover insights on a national level, and integrates that data into marketing decisions in their vicinity.

Case 3 – Major Movie Studio Accurately Predicts Weekend Box Office Numbers

The Client

Movie studios have been experimenting with Internet marketing for quite some time. This major film studio was interested in gathering information online to build a library of web and social media monitoring data that could be dissected for many uses.

The Challenge

The studio was interested in tracking online buzz about specific films to see if there was a correlation between online mentions and box office receipts from a movie's opening weekend.

How They Utilized Social Media Monitoring

Based on long-term data benchmarks from Spiral16, the studio created a formula to accurately predict first weekend box office numbers by measuring the volume of online discussion around specific movie titles. By benchmarking against their own release schedules and the release schedule from rival studios, the studio developed formulas to accurately predict its films' opening weekend box office revenues and adjust marketing initiatives as needed. The studio started tracking online traffic from the official launch of a film's promotional trailer up to the date it was released in movie theaters.

By tracking competitors' films and opening dates in similar genres, the studio was able to create benchmarks. For example, a competitor's special effects-driven science-fiction film with an A-list movie star was monitored during the Christmas holiday season leading up to its release. The following year, the studio released a similar picture at the same time.

Comparative data sets measuring the volume of online chatter, web page links, and sentiment were also collected for romantic comedies, animated films, action movies, and thrillers. Each study was correlated with offline metrics such as past box office performance, yearly and seasonal box office grosses; and theatrical release dates.

The studio gained the ability to adjust promotions to increase revenue and developed a matrix to determine marketing budgets by integrating social metrics with sales data.

Why This Matters for Your Business

Web and social media monitoring platforms are business intelligence tools for today's rapidly changing environment. These advanced technologies enable companies to answer questions that traditional data cannot answer. The important thing is to ask the right questions. Once companies have collected the relevant online data, it can be exported into customized sets of metrics that are germane to your business and help with decision making on an ongoing basis.

Using Social Media Monitoring to Research and Engage New Customers

Forrester Research has stated social media is the fastest-growing segment in interactive marketing. According to Advertising Age, the auto industry alone is expected to spend $4.6 billion on social media marketing by 2015. But even with the jaw-dropping growth of social media and the growing importance of monitoring social media and the web, many brands still aren't sure how to use monitoring / listening platforms for their business. Social media monitoring gives companies the ability to tap into the web, which is the world's largest unstructured data set. One of the many ways social media monitoring benefits clients is to gain information that can be utilized for new business development or to research market expansion.

Case 4 – Hunting and Fishing TV Show Used Web and Social Media Monitoring to Research New Market and Engage New Customers

The Client

America's longest-running hunting and fishing television program is a very popular syndicated series that has been on television for over 20 years. The TV programs introduced their own branded line of outdoor products.

The Challenge

The television program was looking to expand into a broader outdoor-activity market for their branded products beyond hunting and fishing. The brand was expanding their line to include products for hiking, kayaking and mountain biking.

How They Used Monitoring

The brand utilized social media monitoring to identify websites and blogs where online discussions about hiking, kayaking, and mountain biking were occurring. The television show's team engaged with the readers of these blogs and websites about their new product lines. Over time, the brand found individuals who were active and influential in the outdoor-activity community online and received valuable feedback about their products.

Case 5 – Ugly Sweater Party

The Ugly Christmas Sweater Party began as a keg party amongst friends at a popular public university in 2004. Years later, the group turned what started out as a silly holiday bash into a benefit for a well known local charitable organization in the inner city.

Since the group wanted the money they raised to stay in the area, nearly everything at the party was donated by local businesses: the venue, beverages, auction items, etc.

This study shows social media monitoring capabilities on a small scale, as well as its use for non-profit purposes. Data was collected from the first day of October through mid-December.

Category Breakdown

Knowing the metropolitan area had a strong social media community; the group used their online contacts to spread the word about the benefit via Twitter, Flickr, Facebook and personal blogs. The information obtained via social media monitoring indicated the Blog and Social Network categories make up over 77 percent of the ecosystem where the Ugly Christmas Sweater Party was mentioned.

- Blogs – 40.11 percent
- Social Networks – 34.07 percent
- Company/Organization – 11.54 percent
- Video – 7.69 percent
- Social Bookmarks – 3.85 percent
- News – 1.65 percent
- Forums – 1.1 percent

News websites only contributed 1.65 percent of the total sites in the ecosystem, meaning that although the benefit event was successful in raising money for the charitable organization, it did not generate much press coverage. In fact, the news organizations that mentioned the party mistakenly used a web link that pointed to the wrong website, instead of to the event's official website – which was the only place where tickets could be purchased for the fund raising event.

Semantic Cloud

The Semantic Cloud lists the most popular words on all of the sites in the ecosystem via social media monitoring queries. The words appear like a tag cloud, with the most frequently used words displayed in a larger type size. Unfortunately, the data showed that the group didn't effectively communicate the purpose for throwing the party. From the Semantic Cloud, the group learned they would need to use different wording in their marketing efforts for the following year's party. The name of the charitable organization did not appear anywhere on the list of the top 100 words; nor did the name of the venue, or the date of the event.

Here are some words that do indicate the positive nature of the party. The percentage next to the word is the amount of sites in the total ecosystem on which the word appears:

- Benefit – 47.3 percent
- Community – 13.4 percent
- Help – 40.7 percent
- Poverty – 15.6 percent

Sentiment

Sentiment is measured in three degrees: Positive, Neutral, and Negative. There were not a lot of reviews about the event, but the ones that were posted were all positive. One local blogger who attended the fund raiser wrote: "If I knew the date for next year's Ugly Sweater Party, I would mark it on my calendar right now. It was such a blast, and awesome knowing that all the money went to the [charity's name] – I think over $5,000 was raised. Incredible!"

This case illustrates how social media monitoring provides valuable insight that enables organizations of all types to listen, learn from mistakes, adapt, and improve to dramatically increase their chances for future success – this should be an ongoing cycle.

Case 6 – Full Menu Movie Theater

The Client

A new movie theater showing first-run films with in-theater dining from an extensive grill menu featuring appetizers, salads, entrees, and desserts; as well as a full-service bar stocked with top-shelf liquors, first-rate red and white wines; and premium bottled and draft beers. Theater patrons have their choice of sitting at reserved two-top tables, at counter seats, or in regular theater seats with built-in trays for dining. At the push of a button, orders are placed with a staff member who serves customer's food and beverages directly to their seats before and during the show.

The Challenge

The theater chain's manager sent out preliminary invitations to bloggers via Twitter. Those who responded received invitations to a special event. Taking photographs and shooting video was encouraged while the bloggers were given a VIP tour of the exciting new facility. The theater chain's goal was to generate local buzz a few days before the theater's grand opening the night of Halloween.

How They Used Monitoring

The social media monitoring query began running the day after the special event for bloggers, three days before Halloween. Since sophisticated monitoring tools like Spiral16's can look back in time, data came in from as far back as June. The search terms specifically mentioned the new theater from some coverage via local newspapers and television news stations during the theater's construction phase.

The day before the event, only 34 websites specifically mentioned the theater. Growth over the few days following the event was extremely impressive:

- 24 hours: 73 sites
- 48 hours: 93 sites
- 72 hours: 155 sites

From October 28 to November 2, the ecosystem grew 80 percent and there were specific mentions of the theater on 168 websites.

Reviewing the results of the social media monitoring query, it was clear the bulk of the ecosystem's growth came from social technology websites:

- Blogs – Posts by three popular regional film critics
- Social networks – Twitter

- Reference sites – Flicker
- Videos – YouTube

These categories combined make up 67 percent of the ecosystem – and were all sites where users can have conversations, exchange and share user-generated content.

It's worth mentioning that just over 24 percent of the ecosystem consisted of News websites. After drilling down to analyze the results, it was discovered most of these sites pulled articles directly from the Associated Press newswire.

Comparing the blog and social network activity the day before the special event for bloggers, to 48 hours after the grand opening, it was evident how user-generated content exploded as soon as the bloggers could get home to their computers. Some of them didn't even wait that long, posting tweets on Twitter via their smartphones from inside the theater!

A few other pieces of information indicated the theater's attempt to combine a "real world" activity with the digital world was very successful. The theater chain's press releases and websites made up less than nine percent of the total ecosystem. The overall sentiment in the ecosystem was overwhelmingly positive. The Sentiment graph indicated only seven percent of the conversations that registered sentiment was neutral or negative. Based on these percentages (company sites and press releases vs. social technology sites), the theater chain's investment for the one night special event of VIP tours for bloggers resulted in 750 percent growth in positive online conversations.

Among the many benefits of persistent listening via social media monitoring is the way it enables direct engagement with consumers. Engaging individuals is absolutely essential for successful social media initiatives!

Chapter 8

ENGAGEMENT

Engagement and Conversations

Since consumers listen to each other much more than they do to organizations, it's futile to lecture to them via "megaphone style" communications through various mediums. Consumers want to be heard and engaged in genuine dialogues. Social media networks are the place for genuine conversations and companies must foster highly-interactive two-way exchanges to build relations with consumers that evolve into a component of a mechanism that continuously builds brand, and eventually enables marketers to go from having mere insight to having actual foresight. The fact consumers spend so much time on social media networks presents very real opportunities for marketers to leverage the ongoing word of mouth into meaningful conversations.

All these dialogues that take place online amongst consumers provide a plethora of pertinent information. Instead of conducting research via antiquated methods like focus groups, marketers need to spend time where consumers are getting their information, and pay very close attention to what they are saying to each other. Companies need to stop pushing their interruptive monologues of outbound communications, and engage consumers by being trustworthy and accountable. Once they establish trust, companies can participate in and facilitate the two-way conversations consumers are having with each other, and provide them with information they're interested in, and with relevant content they'll find compelling.

Waiting to Talk

Many companies involved in social media marketing are going through the motions, but aren't actually engaging consumers in bona fide conversations. Conversations are inherently social. And naturally, conversations are between people. That's a big problem with so many companies' approach to social media – "social" is all about people – real people with real feelings, opinions, families, friends, pets, careers, hobbies, pastimes, etc. Way too many organizations trying to find their way in social media lose sight of this important fact; people are what make it "social" media. It's not just about the social networks. It's about people; consumers are people. Consumers insist they can tell when organizations are feigning interest about what they're actually saying; when in fact the organization is merely paying lip service to consumers by saying they're listening. If organizations are just pretending to listen to what the consumers are saying, that's not a conversation. That's faking it long enough to find an opportunity to spew out another monologue of contrived messages from on high; this is exactly what consumers are tired of and don't want to hear. There is a strong propensity for marketers to use a megaphone, and it's a hard habit to break for some. Take the megaphone and throw it away!

There was a small portion of a scene from the Academy Award-winning film, Pulp Fiction that ended up on the editing room floor. The deleted segment was from when Vincent Vega goes to the house of his boss Marsellus Wallace, to accompany his wife Mia Wallace, out for the evening to take her to do whatever she wants to do. Vincent and Mia had never met prior to this particular evening when Vincent goes to pickup Thurman's character at the Wallace home.

Vincent makes himself a drink as Dusty Springfield, "Son of a Preacher Man" is playing through the home's sound system. (Mia has Vincent take her to Jackrabbit Slim's to eat; then to enter and win the dance contest). In the deleted scene before they leave the house to go out for the evening, Mia asks Vincent some questions to get a feel for what kind of person he is. One of the questions she asks is, "In a conversation, do you listen or wait to talk?" After a long pause while thinking, he replies, "I wait to talk – but I'm trying to listen."

Unfortunately, this isn't true of most companies when it comes to social media marketing. Like Vincent Vega, they're waiting to talk (because they've been doing all the talking for years) it's what they're accustomed to doing.

Ignoring Customers Results in Punishment

At least one study has been conducted on how consumers react to retail companies that ignore the questions and complaints they've posted on social media networks. The results of the study may surprise you. Consumers punish companies that ignore them! The study indicated that nearly 30 percent of consumers who are ignored by companies on social media cause them to become "very angry." Nearly 30 percent (possibly the same respondents from the study) insisted they would altogether stop doing business with the "offending company." It gets worse. Over 60 percent of questions and complaints posted online about retailers go completely ignored. This is partly due to the sheer volume of content posted on sites like Facebook and Twitter. (However, with professional social media monitoring tools and a few people dedicated to listening, readily identifying mentions of their names, brands, or product names wouldn't be problematic). 30 percent of the retail companies that participated in this study admitted they do not respond to questions or complaints posted on social media sites, and choose to ignore issues mentioned on social forums.

Ignoring issues doesn't make the issues go away. Ignoring customers doesn't make them happy; it makes them go elsewhere to be the customer of another company. Engagement is the goal, and ignoring customers is the antithesis of engaging them.

Engagement With Consumers Is The Outcome

The majority of companies involved with social media marketing are dabbling in it, but they don't realize that's the case. They think they're doing the right things and simply don't know better. Their lack of knowledge about what they should be doing is the reason their efforts don't yield the results they expected. Best practices are not difficult to explain, but the proper implementation of them within an organization is a different story. The problem has to do with having the wrong perspective. That is, companies view engagement with consumers as the objective without realizing there's an entire process and series of activities that must occur before engagement with consumers will even come about. The philosophical "disconnect" is like a wide, deep chasm. Companies make engagement the focal point for the end result without realizing how much is required in the way of time, effort and resources for that result to occur – let alone effectively executing along the way.

Engagement with consumers is the desired outcome – the result that occurs from conversations that place all of the concentration on the consumers and their needs. When companies learn to stop talking about their brand, really start listening, (without waiting to talk), and pay rapt attention, an open conversation can take place. Through those ongoing conversations, relationships develop and trust is established. Through those relationships engagements will ensue.

How Jason's Deli Engages Consumers

Here's a great example of someone who understands engagement and has it down to a science. Christina Trapolino manages the brand online via social media for the south Texas-based restaurant chain, Jason's Deli. There are 236 Jason's Deli locations in 28 states across the southern half of the U.S. – from Washington, DC to Southern California. Jason's Deli serves delicious, high quality soups and sandwiches.

Christina manages a simple yet highly effective weekly Twitter promotion for Jason's Deli called, #TuesdayTrivia. Every Tuesday, a food-related trivia question is tweeted from the Jason's Deli Twitter account. The trivia questions aren't related to menu items, nor do they require any knowledge about the company or their restaurants – they are simply about food in general. Anyone can participate and try to win the gift card given away each week, they merely have to type their answer in a tweet that includes @jasonsdeli and #TuesdayTrivia within one hour of the trivia question being posted on Twitter. One of the people who tweets the correct answer to @jasonsdeli *and* includes the #TuesdayTrivia hashtag is selected randomly and wins the gift card. The person who wins is notified via a tweet and instructed to privately provide their name and mailing address via the Jason's Deli website. When the winner responds, they're sent a generous gift card that can be redeemed at any Jason's Deli and a hand-written note thanking them for participating. There's no sales pitch or gimmicks – simply a personal, genuine note of thanks with their gift card.

The genius in this form of engagement is the simplicity.

Christina Trapolino is an online brand management pro. Her use of best social media marketing practices shines through in a couple of ways. First, she does not make the weekly Twitter promotion all about Jason's Deli. In fact, food is the only thing the trivia questions have in common with the restaurants. This makes participation fun for people on Twitter, as they aren't required or even expected to go to a Jason's Deli location or to scour the company's website and learn the menu just to attempt an answer the weekly trivia question. The other great thing Christina does is show restraint. She isn't tempted to lecture through a megaphone, because she doesn't have a megaphone. When Christina sends the hand-written note along with the gift card, the recipients are happily surprised by the warm, personal gesture, and by not receiving a menu, a brochure, the address of the nearest Jason's Deli, or anything of the sort. On behalf of Jason's Deli, Christina Trapolino engages people on a one-to-one basis every week. If those people choose to interact with Jason's Deli, that's great! If they choose not to, that's their prerogative. Either way, Jason's Deli won't be spamming them, or lecturing them about how great their food is, or telling them how they need to hurry into the nearest Jason's Deli today.

Due to the surprise and delight experienced by the gift card recipients, whether or not they actually become customers is somewhat of a mute point. The odds are high these individuals will share their experience with family and friends, thereby generating positive word of mouth for Jason's Deli – unsolicited testimonial via word of mouth is the very best marketing that exists.

The straightforward nature of the weekly Twitter trivia question has another benefit which is particularly noteworthy. Since anyone on Twitter can participate in #TuesdayTrivia, a growing number of tweeps anticipate the trivia question from Jason's Deli on Tuesdays. The Jason's Deli Twitter account doesn't have tens of thousands of followers – actually a modest amount for a restaurant chain with locations from California to the East Coast. Even so, due to the number of retweets of the trivia question tweet and hashtag searches on #TuesdayTrivia, each week, that single tweet from Jason's Deli has a total reach of hundreds of thousands of people on Twitter! This is a testament to the power of social media marketing done properly and the virality made possible by social networks.

The Jason's Deli example is a real world case of a restaurant chain getting impressive results using just one social network. What about an extremely popular entity that's well recognized internationally?

Satisfaction

Two weeks before Mick Jagger's 19th birthday, The Rolling Stones played their very first gig at the Marquee Club on Oxford Street in London, on July 12th 1962. July 12th 2012 marked 50 years since that occasion, and The Stones were releasing a new book titled, "All Down The Line" to commemorate their Golden Anniversary.

Six weeks before their 50th anniversary the band started a worldwide promotion via Twitter. To have a chance to win a free copy of their new book, fans were encouraged to send tweets to @RollingStones and use the hashtag #RollingStones50. Tweets with the #RollingStones50 hashtag poured into @RollingStones in a number of different languages. The Rolling Stones' official Twitter account claims "All tweets come straight from the Tongue and Lips" – a reference to their iconic mouth logo designed by the artist John Pasche in 1971. Each week several fans were randomly chosen and tweets containing the winners' Twitter names were announced by "Tongue and Lips" from the band's official account. The promotion went viral almost instantaneously as retweeting flourished, and @RollingStones "favorited" clever tweets. Traffic to The Stones' Twitter account increased dramatically, along with their number of followers, and other promotions from the band.

The band loaded up their YouTube channel with "authorized content" of vintage footage taken during concert tours from 1972, 1975 and 1981; as well as a handful of very high-quality HD videos from the world's largest concert ever, when The Stones play before an audience of 1.5 million people at Copacabana Beach, Rio De Janeiro, Brazil, in February 2006. Tongue and Lips sent plenty of tweets about subscribing to The Rolling Stones' You Tube channel to view specific songs. Fans also found commercials on their YouTube channel for the 30th anniversary of "Some Girls" which had been re-mastered and re-released as a double CD Collector's Edition, with 12 previously unreleased tracks; and for the 30th anniversary boxed set Collector's Edition of "Some Girls." The commercials on YouTube included links to purchase these items from Amazon in the United States and the United Kingdom, as well as links to buy them directly from the official Rolling Stones online stores in the U.S. and the U.K.

In addition to chances to win the commemorative 50th anniversary book, followers could enter to win apparel from the band's official online store. As Stone's fans became increasingly aware of the store and new T-shirt designs, Tongue and Lips announced discounts of 20 percent off certain items during their "Hot Summer Savings" promotion that ended on Friday, June 22nd. The official Rolling Stones online store allows fans to preorder the 50th anniversary commemorative book, and has everything from a $6,500 pinball machine to a "clearance outlet" section with items priced as low a $3. The online store also sells the band's albums on CD, vinyl, and via digital download. It also offers men's shirts, women's apparel, children's clothing, outerwear, hats and beanies, pet clothing and accessories, snow skis, magnets, key chains, posters, stickers, postcards, buttons and pins, playing cards, trading cards, books, calendars, videos, coffee mugs, pendants, The Rolling Stones Collector's Editions of both the Monopoly, and Trivial Pursuit board games, and gift certificates.

All the buzz about The Rolling Stones 50th anniversary, their commemorative book, and the revenue generated from their official online store during June and July 2012 originated from their presence on Twitter.

Engagement Across Multiple Platforms

Granted, the vast majority of companies don't have a 50 year history of fame and global name recognition like The Rolling Stones. However, even the smallest brands can generate buzz via social media marketing; and it doesn't have to cost a fortune. I'm sure either Mick Jagger or Keith Richards could bankroll an expensive marketing campaign, but they didn't during the Summer of 2012, because a big budget wasn't necessary – sending tweets via Twitter doesn't require much in the way of money. Social media marketing is a great equalizer and levels the playing field for small companies that don't have money to burn like Mick and Keith.

Nascent brands could establish awareness for a new product targeted towards a particular segment of people starting the way a mid-market company like Jason's Deli did on one social network. They should get very creative and engage consumers across multiple platforms.

The brand could post trivia questions via tweets on Twitter about a promotional video which is available to view on YouTube. Participants who want to answer the trivia questions could be instructed to do so on the company's website would, receive limited edition logo apparel like hats and T-shirts that promote the product, win coupons to redeem the product at a discount, and be entered in a contest to win free products. This could all be part of a fully-integrated, multi-platform promotional mix designed to generate interest and develop exposure via word of mouth amongst those who find the brand relevant.

In addition, to help keep the targeted segment of people engaged in the brand, rather than viewing the YouTube video passively, interactive contests could be put into action with an opportunity for viewers to "text to win" by using their ever-present mobile phones, or to answer trivia questions regarding very specific details from an incident that occurred in the promotional YouTube video.

A separate contest could be established to create user generated content in the form of imaginative YouTube videos that promote the brand – people who create videos for YouTube could achieve recognition on the brands' Like page on Facebook.

Furthermore, there should be cross-platform continuity built in so fans can chose the winner of the user generated YouTube videos via the platform they prefer – casting their vote by sharing the link to their favorite video, to a particular e-mail address at the company directly from within YouTube, by using a specific hash tag on Twitter, by sending a certain code via text message to a designated number on the brand's Facebook page, the company's website, or via a mobile phone app. With a solid strategy in place and some bright creative minds, the possibilities are limited only by the lack of imagination.

Chapter 9

CONVERSIONS, METRICS AND ATTRIBUTIONS

Portions of the General Public Transition Into Paying Customers

A funnel is commonly utilized to depict the approach for the sales process. The goal for the selling team is to move people down the funnel. At the wide mouth at top of the funnel there are prospects, going down the funnel initial contact is made, sales leads are next, followed by identifying the needs of the sales lead, which determines if the sales lead is qualified – the funnel continues to narrow. Moving further down the next steps are presenting a proposal, followed by negotiations, and finally closing the sale which results in a deal transaction and the acquisition of a new customer.

Funnels are used to illustrate a marketing process as well. At the top of the funnel is a specific marketing campaign. The next level down is consumer awareness; followed by interest. The funnel narrows as those who are interested show desire and may or may not evaluate the product or service. At the bottom of the funnel is action on the part of the consumer. In many cases this action is a purchase made by the consumer; and with more complex and higher priced products or services, the bottom of the marketing funnel feeds into the Sales Funnel explained above providing prospects and leads to the selling team.

Social Media Funnel

Since the funnel concept is familiar, it will be used here to represent the approach for social media marketing.

Envision a funnel.

The top of the funnel can represent consumers as a mass, or a particular audience segment your company is trying to target. Naturally the aim is to move people down the funnel – each step is a conversion. With social media monitoring and listening platform software tools, each segment of the funnel can be measured, starting with the people who become fans, Like your Facebook page, circle your organization on Google+, follow your company on Twitter, LinkedIn, or Pinterest.

Conversion Points

Once a person becomes a fan they can be engaged. The next step is to attempt to get the fans to provide contact information like their e-mail address so they can subscribe to your company newsletter; for instance. Obtaining contact information is another conversion that can be measured. The contact information should be utilized for more engagement to attract the fan with offers that are relevant to them so they move further down the funnel and get closer to becoming customers.

The next measureable conversion point is the number of people who acted on the offering by completing an online survey, downloading an eBook or White Paper, sending a text message to the number you provide, or an e-mail to a specific address. The people who respond to offers are definitely showing interest and are moving down the funnel. It is important to understand how continually monitoring and listening enables your company to look at conversion rates, comparing them to messaging and offers you have made over time, so ongoing tweaks can be made for constant improvement that lead to more conversions. This requires careful analysis of trends – the data won't jump up and down and wave at you. However, the data is available via the analytics that come via the social media monitoring tools. Assuming the necessary time and effort is dedicated to reviewing the data; spikes in conversion rates will be identifiable. Those spikes can be correlated to the offers, invitations, and messaging used at the times when there were noticeable increases in conversion rates. Persistent use of monitoring and listening tools allows constant learning so adjustments can be made to increasingly improve and generate better results from each separate social media initiative. This isn't easy but the upshot makes it well worthwhile – and it is definitely a best practice in social media marketing.

The next conversion is when did people who showed interest become actual customers and make purchases. Although knowing when a sale is made isn't difficult to track, the monitoring and listening must continue with customers. An exciting discovery and conversion is when specific customers are identified as people who are saying positive things about your brand or company, and are talking to other people via their social networks. These loyal customers are brand advocates and are extremely valuable to your company. Once a brand advocate has been identified, it is a best practice to recognize them as such, engage them, and empower them to speak on behalf of your brand or company.

Many CEOs and members of the C-Suite shudder at the very idea of having outsiders speak on behalf of their brand and push back hard regarding their company having any sort of social media presence; they want the messaging to come from marketing like it always did. The fact of the matter is people talk to each other about the good and bad experiences they have with companies and are going to continue to do so whether or not the company they're talking about has a social media presence. Since so many senior-level marketers are struggling to get their heads around how to push forward with social media marketing, it stands to reason that CEOs and other members of the C-Suite have their heels dug in hard.

However, there are a few facts about social media that are self evident. Social media has dramatically changed the landscape for businesses and brought about a great deal of change for marketers. It has also leveled the playing field for small businesses, allowing them to obtain a share of voice they'd never have the financial resources to achieve in the pre-social media era. Another truth about social media and all that comes with it, (whether those things are perceived as good or bad), is it's here to stay. Social media is still growing at a swift pace and its use is practically ubiquitous on devices across the world. Social media has led to social media marketing, which has led to social commerce.

Although it's easier said than done, the aforementioned CEOs need to "let go" and roll with the changes. The world has changed and businesses must change along with it and adapt to the way things are now. Living in the past and yearning for the way things used to be won't do a thing to drive the company forward. One of the mottos frequently used by the United States Marine Corps could be taken to heart as good advice for those who are resisting with their heels firmly dug in. That motto is: Adapt. Improvise. Overcome.

Data from Conversions

Measuring the various points of conversion enables a company to look back and calculate the percentage of fans that became customers, and the number of customers that became brand advocates. Determining what correlations exist can provide benchmarks and insight, like how many fans would be needed to land 20 new customers. Tracking all the data across each segment within the social media funnel over time will reveal trends that allow modifications to offers and fine-tuning to messaging that resonate well within each segment.

Ascertain Tracking Methods for Victories

Google Analytics is an excellent tool for tracking information pertaining to website traffic, including numbers of visitors, locations of visitors on a level as granular as the name of the city, percentage of new visitors, percentage of returning visitors, amount of time spent on the site, number of page views, bounce rate, which pages were viewed, sources of traffic, percentage of direct traffic, percentage of traffic sources from referring sites and search engines, which search engines were utilized, specific keywords used for traffic derived via search engines, etc.

Reach and influence via Twitter can be gauged by tools like Twitalyzer, Twinfluence, and Social Bro.

Google+ Ripples enables one to see who publicly shared a post via Google+ and the comments they have made, how the post was shared over time, as well as statistics regarding how a post was shared. Google+ Ripples does this by creating an interactive graph of public shares of any public posts on Google+ to depict the way a post "rippled" through Google's social media platform. This information is useful for discovering new and interesting people to follow.

Facebook "Like" Pages include the ability to examine page Insights to view the number of new likes, lifetime likes, monthly active users, weekly active users, and daily active users. This information can be viewed at a more detailed level to see dates when new likes or unlikes took place, and demographic data including gender, age, and country location. In addition, Facebook's Insights reveal external sites from where people were referred and well as the dates and amount of media consumed from a Like Page, including the number of audio listens, the number of videos and photos viewed.

Depending on your organization's specific objectives, the metrics mentioned above should be interpreted to determine which social media marketing campaigns are most effective and merit further investment, and which have underperformed and should be curbed.

Metrics

Keeping track of the number of fans and followers is important because it's an important point of social media marketing. Viewing the number of fans and followers on a standalone basis isn't particularly valuable and must be put into context. These numbers serve as a point of reference to develop an understanding of how monthly increases in fans and followers on each social network compares to leads coming into the company via traditional channels. Pairing this information with internal data can provide insight and correlations to the growth of a company's business overall, and ratios that exist between social media marketing initiatives and other initiatives in the marketing mix.

All companies want more fans and followers, but increases in those numbers don't mean much if fans and followers aren't converted to provide contact information, show interest, and eventually become customers. While it all begins with obtaining fans and followers, moving these people down the funnel is the goal. Seeing the areas of the funnel where conversions are sluggish is a clear signal where messaging, offers, and calls to action need to be reassessed and modified.

Constant monitoring over time provides metrics enabling companies to know the average conversion rate of fans and followers becoming paying customers. As a result the company has determined their conversion rate is X percent.

Why stop there?

Using X percent as a gauge for conversions up to that point in time, continual engagement, monitoring and listening, will help provide the knowledge needed to increase the conversion rate by another percent over time, and eventually by yet another percent. This knowledge helps reveal companies' strong points and weak points and enables insight into where adjustments need to be made. In some cases, the adjustments involve continual fine-tuning, while in other instances there may need to be changes in the overall strategy.

Demographics

It's important to understand who your customers are, from where they originate, and what method of social media they utilized to become a follower or a fan of your company.

Fans and followers are likely to come from very wide areas and be diverse in nature. Understanding the demographics of these people is necessary to see if they are indicative of the types of people you are attempting to reach. I purposely avoided the popular marketing term, "target audience" because these people should be thought of as just that; people. While they are indeed your target audience, the term is rather dehumanizing. The very nature of social media marketing is about being social, connecting with and engaging people as individuals – get in the habit of thinking of them that way. The more you're able to learn about these people the more relevant your messaging can be (so it resonates with him or her); in turn the more likely they are to move down the funnel to become customers and highly coveted brand advocates. Using analytics tools in Facebook and Twitter will provide data to help you understand the primary demographics of fans and followers. This information should be compared with what you know about your existing customers to determine if new fans and followers originate from the same places as your customer base.

Demographics have always been an important part of marketing, and with social media marketing as a component of a company's marketing mix, demographics are still every bit as significant. If your company is engaged in a social media marketing campaign on Twitter directed towards men in the 24-49 age demographic and you're experiencing a continuous surge in fans and followers of women on Facebook in the burgeoning 55+ age demographic, clearly your messaging is way off the mark and needs to be remedied right away. This type of realization would require more than fine-tuning or minor adjustments. Naturally, the offerings that men between the ages of 24 and 49 find appealing are going to be different than that of women 55 and older. In addition, developing the best possible understanding of your fans and followers provides appropriate calls to action.

When it comes to a spike in fans and followers it's noteworthy to keep things in the proper context and resist making knee-jerk reactions. I must stress how essential it is to measure social campaigns over time – single data points examined in a vacuum don't reveal anything. A stand-alone snapshot of the number of fans and followers you have today isn't analytical and provides no insight per se.

Maintaining Perspective on Fans and Followers

Here's an example regarding a surge in fans and followers to provide perspective. Let's say as part of a campaign to build brand awareness your company is rapidly gaining new fans and followers because of your "Enter to Win" sweepstakes where you'll be giving away three Amazon Kindle Fire mobile tablets via a random drawing for the people who became a fan or follower during a 30 day campaign. The

Amazon Kindle Fire is extremely popular and is appealing to a variety of different types of people of all ages. Such a campaign could cause a huge surge of fans or followers and possibly triple or quadruple the size of your existing fan / follower base. However, over the weeks that trails the 30 day campaign your base of fans and followers will dwindle simply because people wanted an opportunity to win a free Amazon Kindle Fire, but were never truly interested in your company or brand. Two out of three consumers follow brands on social media sites with the expectation of receiving eligibility for exclusive offers.

With that in mind, it would be naïve to think people would not enter to win something for free that they deem valuable even if they don't value what your company offers. Seeing a big spike after the aforementioned promotion is to be expected and shouldn't cause exhilaration. The spike will in fact drop off following the promotion, and that decline in fans and followers doesn't necessitate retooling your messaging. After the dust has settled during the period subsequent to your company's free giveaway promotion there should be a net increase in bona fide fans and followers who are genuinely interested. It's important to understand who the actual fans and followers are by measuring the people in your social media funnel over time so you can identify those who are likely to convert and move to the next level down the funnel. After the net gain in fans and followers, if the average conversion rates throughout the funnel don't persist, fine-tuning messages would be prudent.

Conversion Analytics

Tracking people from when they become fans or followers to paying customers is an intricate process. This is because of the considerable gap between the top of the social media funnel down to where the funnel narrows to the point where a purchase transpires. At the top of

101

the funnel is where companies utilize various forms of marketing to attract people to become fans or followers. Although, the types of marketing and social media that build awareness and cause people to become interested does not typically result in the generation of revenue. The initial intention is to herd large numbers of people into the top of the funnel. Engaging fans and followers and building relationships with them moves a percentage of these people down the funnel via various conversions, which results in some of them becoming actually customers who spend money on the companies' products or services. The further people are down the funnel the closer their proximity to making a purchase. People at the top of the funnel who recently became aware, and are now fans or followers are quite some distance from being paying customers, except on some occasions.

For example, such an instance occurs when the person who becomes aware of a company's product and is already interested in a particular item, conducts a Google search to find it. During their search, they find the specific item they desire, make a quick decision, and fortuitously immediately purchase the item from your company.

Attributions

Measuring social media investments and the effect on revenue can be achieved by tracking multiple touch points made by fans and followers. Tracking all of people's touch points allows companies to attribute where conversions occur and what social media content or offers led to various conversions. The careful examination of analytics provides a representation of how social media marketing initiatives impact revenue and provide valuable insight.

Metrics to measure regarding social media content include – number of conversions, conversion rates through the funnel, revenue per conversion, and total revenue generated by each social media marketing initiative. These KPIs are important to companies of all sizes and can be measured to granular levels. While this degree of measurement is possible, it isn't always necessary. It's important to focus on the KPIs and measure what matters to your organization. The fact that so many things can be measured doesn't mean all those things should be measured.

You may have seen a youngster playing with a retractable tape measure for the first time, or may have done this yourself as a child. This novel new "toy" is fun, and the measurements are excitedly reported to the child's parents. Mom and dad may learn a 2 liter bottle of soda is 12 inches tall, the lid on the jar on peanut butter in the pantry is 3½ inches across, the plastic souvenir cup from the football game is 5½ inches tall, the ironing board is 53 inches long, the case their child's Sony PS3 game came in is 5 inches wide and not quite 7 inches long; and a saltine cracker measures exactly 2 inches on one side, but is a little less than 2 inches on the other side. This is all very interesting to the child, and the parents are pleased with their child's curiosity and the realization that everything can be measured, but the length of the ironing board isn't information truly of interest to mom or dad.

Measuring Relevant Information

Measuring irrelevant information just because you can is a waste of time and resources – keep from getting overly enamored with measurement. Focusing on the most pertinent matters will keep you on track. Clearly define the strategies for calls to action. Closely monitor which offers are working well and leading to conversions. Make effective use of different landing pages that are tailored to the specific link a person followed to arrive on your site so the messaging, call to action, or offer are highly relevant. Create as many unique landing pages with separate content as are necessary.

Note: While creating various landing pages for specific links to help understand attributions, be certain to welcome visitors that arrive at each landing page and acknowledge where that visitor came from to increase relevance and show appreciation. For instance, if you create a short URL and use it in a tweet, people who arrive on the landing page dedicated to that shortened URL should be greeted accordingly. "Thank you for jumping over from Twitter to check out this week's sale items!" The same goes for QR codes. Since every QR code can be completely unique, using warm greetings are perfect when using these codes in print ads or on collateral pieces. "Thank you for using the QR code on our ad in the April issue of Vogue to visit our site. Congratulations! We're offering 15 percent off our new line of sandals as our way of saying "Thank You" for checking our site via the ad you're looking at now." Let's say you generate a QR code that will be placed in an actual location outdoors, like the Third Street Promenade in Santa Monica. "Thanks for using the QR Code at Third and Broadway to visit our site. We're glad you're here! Hope you were able to enjoy some of the great street musicians while on the Promenade."

Understanding Conversions and Attributions Ensures Effective Resource Allocation

Measuring the actions taken by fans and followers all the way through conversions will show how higher conversion rates lead to increases in revenue, and where increases in revenue resulted from swells in revenue that can be attributed to particular conversions. These measurements will also shed light on where decreases in revenue resulted from – reductions in revenue per conversion, from poor conversion rates, or possibly from a combination of both.

Measuring and tracking all the way through the entire funnel indicates where social media investments should be enlarged because of the success attributed to specific social media initiatives, and where those investments should be dialed back in instances where a particular social media initiative did not produce the desired results.

Relevant Measurement Requires Using the Proper Tools

Google Analytics is a powerful tools for developing an understanding of the locations of visitors who visit your website, sources from where the traffic originated, how many pages within the site were visited, how long people spent on any given page, the number of new visitors, returning visitors, bounce rate, etc. I'm a big fan of Google Analytics, use it regularly, and highly recommend it. However, as a web analytics program it can't be used to track analytics like the conversions mentioned in the paragraphs above and wasn't designed for that purpose.

To look above and beyond the realm of website to track a fan, follower, or disgruntled customer who posted a wonderful compliment or nasty comment back to a specific blog page or one unique tweet, requires social media monitoring / listening platform software that provides the sophisticated tools for analytics with this important level of granularity.

Let's Get It Started

It's never too early to start tracking and measuring to make adjustments and improvements. Having a few thousand fans and followers isn't a large enough data set to provide a great deal of insight compared to a company with a few hundred thousand fans and followers. However, with some strategic inbound marketing efforts, as well as continually creating compelling content and sharing that content on social networks, a few thousand fans and followers will continually grow into a sizeable group. Commencing with tracking as early as possible improves proficiencies in tweaking and fine-tuning going forward.

Chapter 10

BRAND ADVOCATES

Identifying Brand Advocates

People on social networks communicate at various levels within the specific communities they choose and identify with the most. Some people are observers. Others yearn for a sense of belonging and find gratification in sharing experiences with others who are like minded and have similar values. The most committed communicators on social networks dedicate considerable amounts of their time and energy pontificating to other members in their group who share the passion about the given topics, causes, brands, and companies. Persistent listening through social media monitoring allows brand loyalists and ambassadors to be identified.

Identifying these highly enthusiastic individuals enables organizations to officially recognize them as "Brand Advocates." These people who are influential in their social networks should be encouraged to disperse information on behalf of the organization via their preferred digital medium, and literally be recognized for their word of mouth efforts. What's more, not only should these highly energized groups be embraced by organizations, organizations should make concerted efforts to facilitate interaction between these people who voluntarily serve as evangelists. Forward thinking organizations realize the value; this vast level of word of mouth builds awareness about product and service offerings, political campaigns, events, and charitable and other benevolent causes.

In addition, organizations who readily engage these groups of people can benefit greatly by collaborating with them in mass, so their collective wisdom can be tapped into for developing new ideas to enhance offerings, devise improved processes, and conceptualize strategies. Organizations desirous of completely embracing best practices in social media marketing need to understand they must not only engage consumers in their brands, but fully empower their brand loyalists as brand advocates.

Brand Advocacy Strategies

What's more, organizations must develop strategies to create advocates for their brands and causes. These individuals are already saying positive things about your brand – marketing departments need to take an active role in growing the number of advocates and energizing them as well. Since consumers don't enjoy talking to corporations, but like talking to other people, advocates should be recognized and identified so consumers can relate to them as individuals with their own unique personalities. Inviting loyal fans and followers to events is an excellent way to turn brand loyalists into advocates. Sending "snail" mail goes a long way too. It's remarkable how effective simple thank you notes are with people. Sending gift certificates, coupons, books, a sample product to try, are all ways to engage and energize loyal followers and encourage them to become brand advocates.

It's all about connecting, forming relationships, and reinforcing the loyalty these individuals have demonstrated via the positive sentiments they've shared on the social web. It's not about spamming or trying to sell them anything – forming relationships is the key here.

Brand Advocates Want to Help Others

Primary research I conducted in 2008 indicated brand advocates had an average of 80 people in their social networks; Millennials had larger social networks. At that time, a primary driver for recommending specific brands was the desire for others to know the brand advocate was very knowledgeable about certain types of products or about an industry niche. This was particularly true of brand advocates amongst the Millennial Generation – they craved recognition and validation from their online peer group.

Today, brand advocates are considerably more altruistic, and only a few percent want others to know about their knowledge. Now the main reason for brand advocates to make recommendations is based on their yearning to help other people, (total strangers), and inform them about the positive experiences they had with a product or service. Over 35 percent of brand advocates make recommendations because they hope it will enable their friends to make more intelligent buying decisions. Less than 10 percent volunteer recommendations for products and services, doing so only when they're asked for their opinion. Only one percent of brand advocates make recommendations because they are incented with rewards like free products and discounts from the companies they recommend. This validates how the underlying motivation of brand advocates has changed over time, and how they've become much more charitable with their recommendations.

How Brand Advocates Make Recommendations

The majority of online brand advocates make their recommendations via e-mail; over 55 percent. 35 percent make their recommendations on Facebook. LinkedIn, Twitter, and blogs combined represent only three percent of where brand advocates make their recommendations. The remaining seven percent of recommendations made are spread across e-commerce and third-party sites like, Amazon, and Yelp. An interesting note is how online brand advocates make recommendations offline as well. In fact, nearly half of their recommendations are made during meetings, while having coffee, during dinner conversations, and while on the telephone.

Brand Advocates and Their Social Networks

In contrast to the 80 or so people brand advocates had in their social networks in 2008 who recommended about three brands, today most brand advocates have between 200 – 450 people in their social networks; nearly 20 percent have over 500 people. Brand advocates who make their recommendations online typically have 300 – 600 people in their social networks. Previously, recommendations made by Brand Advocates were primarily limited to smartphones, beverages, and restaurants. More than two-thirds of brand advocates now recommend products and services for consumers and businesses alike across a multitude of industries.

The Technology industry receives the most recommendations, at 25 percent. Restaurants & Dining receive 15 percent of recommendations from brand advocates, followed closely by Entertainment & Leisure. Household Items, Food, Beverage & Tobacco, each receive 10 percent of recommendations; Health & Fitness, and Travel & Hospitality both receive seven percent. Automotive, Fashion & Apparel, and Beauty & Cosmetics each receive four percent of recommendations from brand advocates.

On the average twenty-six recommendations are made per year by brand advocates. Although nearly 20 percent of brand advocates make a recommendation every week, and nearly 10 percent make several recommendations weekly. What's more, over 15 percent of brand advocates recommend 10 or more brands, products and services, while another 15 percent recommend more than 15 brands!

Super Brand Advocates

Overall, brand advocates are increasingly more active with their recommendations, and approximately 15 percent are extremely active. These "Super Brand Advocates" have over 500 people in their social networks, make several recommendations weekly without any compensation, and recommend over a dozen separate brands, products or services. These recommendations made by super brand advocates are persuasive and have a great deal of influence on billions of dollars of purchasing decisions for everything from trucks to tablet computers, anti-virus software to antipasto salad, and from hotels to hand towels.

It's imperative to have a solid strategy, and the necessary social monitoring and listening platform tools in place to identify your organization's brand advocates!

Why Are Brand Advocates So Important?

The unpaid publicity about brands that is created by users is known as "earned media." Recommendations made by brand advocates are highly valuable to brands because their recommendations lead to more recommendations between trusted friends. This earned media via recommendations is a key benefit social media marketing delivers. Brand advocates sow seeds that create earned media – consumers propagate the recommendations on an enormous scale. The more earned media a brand is able to help generate via brand advocates and engagement with fans and followers on social networks, the more lift brands will see in positive impacts on purchasing behavior due to consumers being exposed to the earned media. Increases in purchases typically occur within a matter of weeks of consumers being exposed to earned media. These increases provide ROI that can be directly attributed to social media marketing. In fact, research analysts estimate every dollar spent identifying and energizing brand advocates results in at least $10 in positive word of mouth impressions and sales.

When brand advocates proactively recommend their favorite brands, products, services, and causes online and offline without being paid to do so, their recommendations are amplified by social media. The reach of these amplified recommendations rivals the reach of advertising, but unlike advertising these recommendations resonate with people as being considerably more trustworthy.

Consumers Are Listening to Each Other

The rapidly escalating tempo to keep up with ever-increasing business complexity is going to continue like the world has never seen before. In this "always on" world of transparency, continual connectivity, information is constantly available, and enthusiastically shared amongst the staggering number of consumers who are engaged online. In the United States, consumers post tens of millions of online product reviews on a weekly basis. These reviews recently became the top influencer for buying decisions for American consumers.

What's more, these online reviews wield nearly twice the level of influence as traditional advertising.

Please take a second to let that fully sink in...

That's right. Online reviews posted by total strangers are nearly twice as effective at influencing what a person decides to buy, than what companies are saying in their ad campaigns.

A Matter of Trust

Consumers trust each other much more than they trust corporations and brands. When it comes to Americans, here's a snapshot of the percentage of consumers who have at least some trust in the following:

- Forty-nine percent trust paid ads in the right column and at the top of search engines
- Online advertising is trusted by 33 percent
- Twenty-eight percent trust unsolicited e-mails from companies or brands
- Eighteen percent trust bloggers and general blog sites
- Only 16 percent trust corporate blogs

One of the world's 10 largest public relations firms, Chicago-based, Edelman, publishes an annual Trust Barometer. (**Disclosure:** During 2006-2007 I was retained on a consulting basis by the Business and Technology practice at Edelman Public Relations Worldwide at their corporate office in Chicago). Over the last handful of years the Edelman Trust Barometer has shown Americans trust has dropped considerably in television news, radio news, newspapers, and even in the level of trust people have in their peers. Separate research indicates (compared to the level of trust Americans have today) the overall level in the United States has dropped precipitously since the 1960s. Even so, 90 percent of American consumers still trust their peers for brand recommendations. Nothing ranks higher. In fact, nothing even comes close!

While it may be a bitter pill to swallow, it is high time companies come to grips with the fact consumers aren't listening to brands like they once did – they're listening to each other via word of mouth. Positive word of mouth is extremely powerful. It's often referred to as "buzz" – and this buzz – the interaction of consumers and users of products or services, dramatically amplifies companies' marketing efforts.

An Energized Brand Advocate

I have a friend in Texas who is a brand advocate for a company that specializes in marketing stimulant-free, liquid multivitamins, minerals, and glucosamine supplements that are used by over 200 professional sports teams and university athletic programs.

Chrissy believes in physical fitness, exercises and lifts weights daily, and prepares healthy, nutritious, balanced meals for her husband, children, and herself. She was already a customer and the company recognized she was actively spreading the word about their products. The company approached her and she became their very first brand advocate. The firm has a brand advocacy program in place and is adding more people regularly – with the goal of having a total of 100 brand advocates in place.

Initially Chrissy was asked to comment on the brands' Facebook page and on Twitter on a regular basis, but to be rather low key. Her role grew into becoming a guest blogger, sending introductory e-mails, and attending client meetings. Along with other ambassadors, photographs of Chrissy will be utilized in the company's marketing rather than professional models.

One of the benefits of this company's supplements is their great taste, and Chrissy receives free product to create recipes that include the supplements. These recipes are published as content and sent to customers. Finally, ambassadors are asked to actively be on the lookout for other customers who seem to fit a specific profile and might want to become brand ambassadors too.

Return on Advocacy

Numerous studies indicate consumers trust word of mouth many times more than advertising and other forms of marketing. As a satisfied customer, Chrissy has become a channel for the multivitamin supplement company's marketing communications. The positive word of mouth generated by active brand supporters like Chrissy results in conversion rates much higher than other forms of marketing because of the "trust factor" associated with her recommendations. Naturally, there are some expenses involved in developing and maintaining a cohesive brand advocacy program. Although, these expenses are low considering the value these efforts return; and very low compared to the expenses incurred for advertising and other forms of paid media.

Another return on advocacy is the way earned media generated by brand advocates lingers on the social web, continuously delivering brands with enduring value from the positive word of mouth. Recommendations from brand advocates posted on the social web can also result in higher page rankings with search engines as well.

Fans and followers may come and go, but brand advocates happily carry on disseminating positive word of mouth about their favorite brands year after year. Some popular American brands actually have "Lifetime Advocates." There's an incredibly large group of people who have been recommending Apple's products since the Apple IIe was released in 1983. Harley-Davidson is another American brand that has super brand advocates who have been recommending the companies' motorcycles for decades.

Brand Advocacy Is Effective For All Types of Businesses

You don't have to have a major brand to have highly-satisfied customers who would be willing to be brand advocates. You must resist negative thinking regarding your brand being too commonplace, or that it isn't alluring enough to talk about. There's even brand advocacy for automobile windshield repair – hardly a business niche that gets a lot of buzz like Apple or Harley-Davidson. If your car's windshield gets chipped or cracked it will need to be repaired – windshield repair companies have passive customers and highly-satisfied customers. Consumers purchase mundane products and services every day. Surveys of over three million American consumers revealed that half the customers of both B2C and B2B companies would consider being unpaid brand advocates. These surveys indicate brand advocates have many times more positive impact on purchasing decisions than famous paid endorsers and spokespeople. The reason is simple – it's a matter of trust.

With a typical survey card that utilizes a ranking of zero to 10, (where zero represents "Would Not Recommend" and 10 represents "Very Likely"), you can learn from your customers by asking them: "How likely are you to recommend our brand / product / service to friends and family?" Customers who return survey cards marked 9 or 10 are clearly indicating their high level of satisfaction, and are excellent candidates for your brand advocacy program.

Forward thinking, adaptive marketers are leveraging the extremely cost-effective and trustworthy marketing communications channel comprised of brand advocates to propel brands and generate results.

Chapter 11

WORD OF MOUTH

Brand Advocates Drive Word of Mouth

Brand advocates are vital to social media marketing strategies because of the word of mouth (WoM) they generate. Positive WoM is the most coveted form of marketing because of the inherent credibility that comes with it. When satisfied customers tell other people how much they like a business, product, service, brand, or event, they put their reputations on the line every time they make a recommendation. Others typically know the people making recommendations don't stand to gain personally by promoting something, therein lies the credibility.

How much credibility?

Here's some important information to provide the proper context:

- Every day in the United States over three billion brand mentions occur in nearly 4½ billion conversations
- Ninety percent of the conversations regarding brand happen offline via face-to-face conversation, or voice-to-voice conversations
- Approximately 70 percent of Americans trust online reviews
- Nearly 80 percent of Americans trust online reviews about hotels and travel
- 4.3 out of 5 stars is the average rating for online reviews of products and services in the United States

- Specific brand names are mentioned 60 times weekly in online and offline conversations by typical Americans
- The majority of conversations taking place around a specific product or service are positive. The chances are good if an individual is talking about your brand, they're saying something good
- Two-thirds of WoM conversations related to a brand are primarily positive
- Less than 10 percent of WoM conversations pertaining to a brand are primarily negative

What Did They Say?

Consumers become engrossed in hearing about new products that are of interest to them, and pay close attention to what other people are saying about these products. Surveys conducted with over 10,000 American social media users indicated that over 75 percent of these consumers are more likely to try new things based on suggestions they learned via social media. Over 70 percent of these consumers are more apt to get on the bandwagon and encourage their friends to try new products. In addition, 55 percent of recommendations made by consumers are based specifically on the customer service experience they had with a company. And nearly 30 percent of consumers are willing to pay 15 percent *or more* to outstanding customer experiences. Clearly, that extra 15 percent could do wonders for increasing earnings.

In September 2012, published research conducted by economists at the University of California-Berkeley found that a half-star improvement on Yelp's 5-star rating made a restaurant between 30 - 49 percent more likely to reach maximum seating capacity during evenings. The researchers at Berkeley concluded online reviews played an increased importance in the consumers' judgment of the quality of products and services.

Word of Mouth is the Most Influential Driver of Purchasing Decisions

Word of Mouth is the by far the number one most influential driver of purchasing decisions for nearly all categories of products and services. According to the global consulting firm, McKinsey & Company, more than 65 percent of the U.S. economy is driven by WoM! Based on the research conducted by Forrester, 500 billion WoM brand impressions are posted daily on the social web. That's about 180 trillion online brand impressions in a single year. Forrester also claims 150 people are reached by each WoM post on the social web. This is attributed to the number of friends people have on social networks like Facebook and Google+, and the number of retweets via Twitter.

It's hard to get one's head around 500 billion word of mouth brand impressions being posted on the social web on a daily basis; 180 trillion annually is mind boggling. What's crystal clear is the powerful benefits inherent to positive WoM via earned media.

Investing in Word of Mouth Marketing is Very Beneficial

While it wasn't referred to as word of mouth marketing at the time, WoM mouth and its inherent influence has been around for ages. Fostering positive word of mouth is a very worthwhile investment. Owned media, (websites, blogs, Twitter and Facebook accounts), paid media, (display advertising, paid search, and sponsorship), are important, but no form of marketing provides greater returns than earned media. Savvy marketers focus on the positive impacts word of mouth marketing can have on the bottom line and brand image.

Word of mouth marketing is inexpensive. Companies can spend as much money on it as they like – companies that execute the best practices in word of mouth marketing focus on the basics – delighting customers with excellent service and experiences. They also create great products and services worth talking about, their representatives are pleasant, they listen persistently, and engage customers in dialogues. Word of mouth marketing saves companies money on advertising, which is expensive, and consumers routinely ignore. Public relations can be quite effective at generating awareness and positioning products, but PR isn't cheap. Occasionally a crisis may occur within a company and PR is required for crisis management to help manage the issue, and overcome the negative word of mouth. However, it's pathetic when companies need to spend money on public relations to overcome negative word of mouth that stems from poor customer service and lackluster customer experiences.

Positive Word of Mouth Saves Organizations Money

Forward thinking companies will save money via the positive word of mouth their happy customers generate, which allows investing in programs and processes that result in even better customer service, more stimulating customer experiences, and more development to enhance products. The more companies can do to give customers great reasons to talk about how thrilled they are, the more this upbeat cycle perpetuates. The outcome is legions of brand loyalists who want to share about their positive experiences. Having delighted customers who find reasons to talk about brands is a competitive advantage smart companies should diligently strive to achieve.

Companies that listen persistently, incorporate relevant feedback via Voice of Customer initiatives to learn about issues, areas that need improvement, and engage their customers in meaningful dialogues – the better suited companies are to glean valuable information from these conversations (information and ideas that wouldn't otherwise come to light). Customers are a fantastic source of new ideas for companies they're loyal to, but only the companies that are engaged and have brand advocacy programs in place are able to benefit from their customers' collective vision. In addition, positive WoM from customers can lead to incremental business for companies. I know of a real world case in the software industry where a delighted customer recommended a software company's product to another company, this resulted in a multi-million dollar contract. Delighted customers don't just recommend consumer products; they are sources for referrals for B2B companies as well.

Keys to Creating Word of Mouth

Vital components to creating positive word of mouth include creating experiences for consumers that are emotional and topical.

We know peers rely on each other as their most trusted resources for recommendations and are well connected via their social networks. Adaptive marketers should leverage social networks to gain access to consumers to generate awareness and build credibility with their brand. Prior to attempting to penetrate a particular segment of people via social networks, savvy marketers should first utilize non-traditional media and events to evoke an emotional response and create relevance in the minds of consumers. Since consumers are increasingly leery of advertising, the combination of mobile tours, on-site promotions, product giveaways and cause marketing can all be utilized to establish mind share and create emotional connections with potential customers.

There's an existing charitable organization I find very worthwhile that is using social media to further their cause. I'll explain what they're doing currently, and then provide valuable information on how they could create the necessary emotional experience to make the organizations efforts more topical and increase WoM.

Case Study: *Water Forward*

I learned about Water Forward via the Virgin website. A goal of Virgin's founder and CEO, Sir Richard Branson, is to create awareness about Water Forward and the billion of people in the world who live without clean water – an ongoing effort to help decrease this number as much as possible. People all across the world are in crisis situations – forced to drink contaminated water which results in literally thousands of deaths a day. Water Forward estimates that every minute three children die from a contaminated water-related illness.

Water Forward believes that with enough funding this crisis can be solved so people drinking contaminated water will have access to clean drinking water. The concept behind Water Forward is to get the billion people around the world with clean water to help the billion without clean water. The idea is a "Pay it Forward" model, where the billion of people around the world that are using social media who have access to clean water, join forces by donating money that support clean water projects around the world – masses of individuals chipping in together should help make this big problem solvable.

Everyone who helps receives recognition in an online book via a "space" that depicts a photograph they upload at the time they make their donation. Each space in the online book costs $10. If a million people donate $10 apiece, $10 million dollars will be generated – enough to help 500,000 people gain access to clean water. When the $10 million goal is achieved, the online book will be made into an actual physical book that will be printed to commemorate its impact, and the book will be placed in a special location, like the Library of Congress in Washington, DC.

The way the pay it forward concept comes into play with Water Forward is you can't buy a space for your photograph in the online book on your own. Someone who has already made a donation and is in the book has to sponsor you by buying a space for a photo; and someone had to sponsor them by buying a space for them so they could get into the book, and so on. Each person with a space in the online book pays it forward to the person or people they sponsor and buy spaces for $10 apiece. Then each person who donates pays it forward to additional people and "nudges" them to donate and buy spaces so the chain of giving perpetuates. Water Forward tracks each person who donated so they can literally see the impact made via their social media connections. There is no limit to the number of people a person can sponsor via $10 spaces in the online book. Each person that enters the book represents progress towards ending the water crisis around the globe.

Water Forward is backed by the New York City-based non-profit organization, charity: water, and 100 percent of all donations go towards building clean water projects in developing countries. charity: water was founded by Scott Harrison in 2006, it has helped raise over $40 million to fund nearly 6,700 projects in 20 countries, benefiting more than 2.5 million people. Private donors, foundations and sponsors fund charity: water's operations and entire infrastructure so 100 percent of all donations go to efforts directly related to the clean water projects. Even the costs associated with credit card transaction fees incurred while making a donation are covered by the generous backers of charity: water. Donations to pay it forward and get into the online book are done through the website, WaterForward.org.

People interested in donating authorize their Facebook or Twitter account to log them into the WaterForward.org website to pay it forward. Richard Branson purchased an enormous number of spaces in the online book to help generate momentum, and I got in directly under him. The spaces he purchased facilitated sponsorship for me and countless others to donate to Water Forward. My donations have purchased spaces for others to claim with their donations so they can pay it forward by purchasing additional spaces, and so on. When donations are made to charity: water, Water Forward provides the ability to spread the word via Facebook or Twitter to inform friends and followers about the water shortage crisis, encourage them to donate money to claim spaces in the online book, and to pay it forward by spreading the word too. Water Forward also provides unique web links that can be pasted into messages so people can spread the same information via e-mail as well.

Combine Online with Offline

It would be great if charity: water's marketing strategy could include a mobile marketing tour with some of the popular brands they've already teamed up with, like KOR Water. KOR is a popular brand that makes BPA-free, unbreakable water bottles that produces the black and yellow, charity: water-branded, KOR Water Delta Hydration Vessels in both 750ml and 500 ml sizes. KOR Water donates the vast majority of their proceeds to the charity: water organization. The "Water Forward Mobile Marketing Tour" could visit several universities across the United States and Canada over a one semester period of time. The on-campus tours would be designed to be highly visible, interactive settings that are free from other media clutter. Together with KOR, Water Forward would generate awareness and create goodwill as teams of brand advocates "advance teams" swarmed their college campuses encouraging fellow students to visit the mobile exhibit, learn about the water crisis, to donate, and do their part to pay it forward to people in need.

charity: water's marketing personnel would have already recruited brand ambassadors on each campus to help build enthusiasm at each school in anticipation of the tour. Via on-campus advertising, students would become aware of the fact that there are 300 million more people in the world with mobile phones than there are people with access to clean drinking water, which would increase concern and word of mouth. The "socially conscious" attitude of Water Forward and KOR would resonate with college students, because socially responsible companies that support charitable causes are deemed highly commendable by Millennials; the tail end of the Millennial Generation that recently finished high school. To reinforce students' generous actions and associate good will with the KOR brand, the on-site exhibits from the mobile tour could have high-definition flat screen televisions with videos demonstrating exactly how 100 percent of their donations would be utilized on well drilling projects that provide access to clean drinking water to people suffering from dehydration, and fatal contaminated water-related illnesses.

In fact, a child dies about every 19 seconds from these illnesses – that's an average of over three deaths per minute. With this new information fresh in students' minds, and without going over the top with gratuitous graphic images of children in such a terrible state, the Water Forward exhibit could simply have the sound of a bell chime quietly every 19 seconds to conjure up the emotional response required to foster WoM about how widespread the problem is and severe the water crisis is around the world. The WaterForward.org website features an informative "How It Works" video that is two minutes sixteen seconds in length. As the video ends, text could appear that reads: "In the time it took you to watch this video, 7 children died from illnesses related to drinking contaminated water." Reinforced by the bell chime every 19 seconds, sensitivity to this tragic situation would invoke emotion, and appeal to students' longing to take action for the greater good. Generally speaking, college students are on tight budgets and may not have $10 to donate.

However, their knowledge of the water crisis should cause them to make the Water Forward project "go viral" and become topical.

Even Better; Utilizing Multiple Platforms

By combining their current activities with offline components that are supported with existing online social media initiatives, charity: water and Water Forward could create more emotional experiences that become topical, and amplify their message so it proliferates via WoM. Marrying social media efforts with live events provides the ability to communicate across multiple channels instantaneously for additional power, reach, and engagement. The combination of offline or In Real Life (IRL) and online elements would enable students to use Twitter to send tweets like, "Watching informative video on @WaterFwd in front of #CampusBookstore," to check in via their smartphones on geo-location social networks like Foursquare, and inspire people to write blog entries that would spread the word about this cause even further.

In preparation for their semester long mobile tour, the marketing personnel at charity: water could identify individuals to recruit volunteer brand ambassadors in targeted geographical regions via the data about specific people that Water Forward already has in their giant online book of those who have already donated and paid it forward. Additionally, retailers in the vicinity of the college campus that carry the KOR brand of water bottles would be encouraged to participate by setting up informative point-of-purchase displays where the KOR water bottles are merchandised on the sales floor. The retail sporting goods, outdoor and camping, bicycling and fitness stores that stock KOR water bottles could benefit by increased foot traffic from students redeeming coupons they received for donating to Water Forward at the exhibit on their campus. Store managers at these specialty stores often will know their clientele and are able to readily identify their most avid and loyal customers to help them spread the word about Water Forward via a flyer with the address and QR code to WaterForward.org. Students who donated $10 for one space might receive a 20 percent off coupon; while students who donated $40 for four spaces might receive a coupon for a free 500ml KOR water bottle.

KOR Water is just one of the many brands supporting the charity: water cause, and happens to be the company I chose for this example. Other brands that have teamed up with charity: water to provide limited-edition branded merchandise, and donate substantial percentages of proceeds to charity: water include: DODOcase, the popular brand that makes iPad cases; GelaSkins, the company that creates protective covers and cases for smartphones, iPods, and laptop computers; Jawbone, who sells the powerful, portable JAMBOX speaker for people on-the-go; tee shirts created by Saks Fifth Avenue; and jewelry, bracelets, hats, hoodies, apparel, and more. With the many cool product offerings from so many companies, the opportunities to create buzz for Water Forward via a combination of online and offline campaigns are substantial.

I learned about Water Forward while on the Virgin website looking for unrelated information. Within minutes of learning about this noble cause, I logged in and purchased a space, and have purchased additional spaces since then. The sad knowledge about three children dying a minute caused me to act immediately. I wondered why I hadn't heard about charity: water and their Water Forward project prior to coming across it via the Virgin website. I purposefully chose this cause as an example of how to combine creative offline marketing and social media marketing in hopes it would help spread the word so others would be inspired to get involved and pay it forward.

Word of Mouth Creates Higher Conversion Rates

WoM marketing campaigns designed to be emotional and topical have a strong propensity to "go viral" very quickly. Because of the level of trust associated with brand advocates, including them in WoM marketing initiatives helps pack a particularly powerful punch. Their enthusiastic recommendations and comments about brands, products, services, and causes, get amplified via social media and extends the reach of the earned media brand advocates helped generate. Due to the level of trust linked to brand advocates, recommendations they initiate result in higher conversion rates than those from traditional paid media.

Compared to conversion rates of one percent or less that result from owned and paid media, conversion rates from earned media are three to five percent and greater. While marketers are spending more on digital marketing in general (with these higher conversion rates in mind), considerably larger portions of marketing budgets need to be specifically allocated to creating earned media via WoM.

Yet companies continue to spend significant portions of their marketing budgets on traditional advertising and paid digital media to generate leads that can easily cost $250 apiece, and clicks that are a couple dollars each. Typically, only a few percent of sales leads are qualified, and companies continue to pay for clicks on search engines – even though 80 percent of click through rates in search engines stem from organic efforts like keyword optimization and meta tags embedded in websites. Only a minuscule portion of marketing dollars spent on paid clicks actually results in paying customers.

Word of Mouth Provides Enduring Value

Earned media via WoM is cost-effective since companies don't pay for the recommendations and positive comments are generated by brand advocates and other satisfied customers. The authenticity associated with this content from trusted sources results in increased conversion rates and higher ROI. Obviously, when positive word of mouth from unpaid brand advocates leads to new paying customers, the ROI is greater than it is from new paying customers acquired via paid advertising, content and owned media. The value created via positive word of mouth is tremendous.

Word of Mouth Helps During a Crisis

Even when a company experiences a crisis, earned media via WoM helps that company weather the storm. A few years ago Toyota had a serious problem with their image when they recalled millions of cars due to unexpected acceleration problems. The repercussions from the news media were significant, and owners of Toyota vehicles went online to seek more information, and to share their aggravation and anxiety. Toyota didn't ignore the crisis, or run and hide. Instead, they acknowledged the severity and scale of the problem utilizing social media to address consumers' valid safety concerns.

In the same way consumers have increasingly less trust in advertising; they'll no longer accept one-sided, prepared press releases either, or a contrived statement that no one on Toyota's executive team was available to make a comment. Now that authenticity and transparency are required to gain consumers' trust, "PR spin" just exasperates problems encountered by companies. Consumers want dialogues and their voices to be heard. Sometimes a crisis will occur – Toyota's crisis was huge.

Wisely, Toyota was very proactive and the company's CEO, Jim Lentz did a live video interview hosted by Digg.com where consumers could submit questions for him to answer. Following the live Q&A session, the company utilized Twitter and the #toyota hashtag to disseminate information and keep the public informed on details regarding the recall.

Toyota's PR team also made use of Twitter to create conversations around their tarnished brand. Even amongst all the disapproval from the public, brand loyalists and brand advocates stood by Toyota and posted tweets about their positive experiences with the company. Years of producing quality products, providing great service, and delivering excellent customer experiences served Toyota well during this crisis situation, as brand advocates came to their aid with unexpected but welcome positive WoM. This real world example of earned media illustrates how WoM through brand advocacy has a lasting value. Not only will highly-satisfied customers make recommendations during the launch of an exciting new product, but will continue to make positive comments about their favorite brands long after their initial purchase – while the brand is experiencing difficulty.

Naturally all of this positive WoM and earned media from unpaid brand advocates isn't completely free. It's in direct correlation with continually providing excellent products and services, outstanding service, and fostering meaningful ongoing dialogues with customers to ensure exceptional experiences that surpass satisfaction and cause delight.

Chapter 12

SOCIAL MEDIA AND ROI

ROI from Social Media Marketing Initiatives

I'll get straight to the point on this. Using the financial metric of return on investment makes it difficult to calculate ROI for social media initiatives. When it comes to measuring ROI, radio, television, print and outdoor ads have always presented a challenge. However, while the method for determining ROI is elusive for social marketing initiatives, it certainly doesn't mean those initiatives are ineffective.

How does an organization calculate the ROI on their CEO's mobile phone or their senior-executive team's e-mail accounts? What about the telephone lines and telephone equipment in a company's Customer Care department or the GPS device in your rental car while driving to a business meeting in a city you've never been to before?

Well-executed social media marketing extends a brand's reach and amplifies other components in the marketing mix. Besides creating brand awareness, brand loyalty can result which can lead to brand equity. Elements included in the valuation of brand equity consist of consumers' recognition of logos and other visual elements, brand language associations made by consumers, and consumers' perceptions of quality. Brand equity can be leveraged to create brand value.

Brand Value

For the last half dozen years, MillwardBrown, a firm that's part of the London-based holding company WPP, publishes their annual BrandZ Top 100 Most Valuable Global Brands report. Their report published in 2012 listed the Top Three companies with staggering brand values in excess of $100 billion: Apple, IBM, and Google. Intangible assets like brand value are extremely advantageous; especially when it comes time to sell the company – and the brand's valuation is calculated and reported on the Balance Sheet. Although these three companies were at the very top of the Top 100 list, even the companies on the bottom of the list had brand valuations in excess of $9 billion – not exactly chump change. Considering the millions of business entities in the world, the Top 100 companies' brand values are hardly indicative of the 99.99+ percent of companies most marketers deal with, yet building brand is still very important.

Brand value is one of the most significant assets a company has and increases the financial value to the organization that owns the brand. As brand value increases an organization should expect to see increases in growth, revenue and earnings which should cause the C-Suite to champion social media marketing initiatives as necessary endeavors for the organization.

C-Suite Members Who Advocate Social Media Collaboration Improve ROI

Many organizations have members of their C-Suite who are not yet convinced social media marketing provides actual business value. Knowing where the organization truly is on this continuum is necessary so rational business cases can be made to the individuals who control the purse strings and approve proposed projects. As you know, many members of the C-Suite tremble at the idea of anyone speaking on behalf of the company other than via the contrived messages created by marketing and their PR team.

Note: Presenting solid information about where the organization is on the continuum provides enlightenment to senior executives – who have little faith in the benefits that come with social marketing - helping them understand where the organization is presently with social initiatives, and where it needs to be. Conveying the budgetary requirements for social marketing efforts, the need for technology and human resources, how those resources will be utilized, and when the organization will be at a point where there will be return on investment and a contribution to earnings (speaking in terms of dollars) is language executives understand and can get their heads around. Articulating such a business case in lucid terms helps put structure around social media initiatives and helps others understand the upside potential social marketing affords – this is especially useful to those who think social media lacks structure and is ethereal. Having support from the C-Suite is extremely beneficial since social media marketing endeavors benefit many areas of a company and needs to be integrated throughout the organization. In addition, when departments work together in a concerted team effort and participate in cross-functional collaboration, the organization realizes higher ROI from social media than organizations that aren't collaborative with their social media endeavors.

Set Attainable Goals

While they are difficult for calculating ROI, all companies benefit by increases in:

- Lead generation
- Brand awareness
- Brand recognition
- Share of Conversation

- Perceived value by consumers
- Customer satisfaction
- Customer loyalty

The business value and benefits from social marketing are all around. They just don't always fit into the mathematical formulas customarily utilized in finance and economics for calculating ROI.

With the organization's goals in mind, it's necessary to realistically assess where the company is at present, where it would like to be, and what the plans are to attain those goals. It is essential social media endeavors are devised to serve as a buttress for the organization's goals. Know where you are, what you hope to attain, and synchronize social media initiatives with those objectives.

Like all goals, they need to be pragmatic and attainable. Social media campaigns are both inexpensive and effective at increasing awareness and sales, so choose precise targets that can be achieved and are completely in line with organizational goals, and tied to a particular period of time.

For example:

- Increase sales by 3.5 percent next quarter
- Increase number of Twitter followers to 20,000 over the next six months
- Obtain 500 followers on Pinterest
- Convert 5 percent of the people who have "Liked" your Facebook page into paying customers during a six week campaign
- Increase number of website page views from five to eight by the end of next month

Focus on Metrics Related to Goals

Instead of the traditional calculation for ROI in monetary terms, evaluate success by measuring KPIs. Keep your focus on the goals set for your organization.

For example:

- Website analytics
- Comments on blog posts
- Insight into consumer sentiment
- Retweets
- Percentage of followers on Facebook who are now customers

How Does Social Media Compare with Traditional Metrics?

Discovering patterns requires filtering through results and plotting them on a timeline. Don't expect the patterns to be readily apparent – a discovery process is required. Review the timeline and look for rises in sales corresponding to the timeframe your social media campaign was running. They won't jump right out at you, but look for other patterns and determine what you can pinpoint that ran in parallel with that particular social marketing initiative.

For instance, are you seeing:

Increases in web traffic?

More page views?

More "click throughs"?

More referrals?

More mentions in blogs?

More followers on Twitter?

More Likes on Facebook?

More people in your company's Circles on Google+?

More pins on Pinterest?

More user-generated videos posted on YouTube?

Large Percentage of Companies Don't Measure ROI

Before we touch on calculating ROI on social media marketing-related endeavors, it's important for you to know something about calculating ROI on marketing in general. This is noteworthy since CEOs and the C-Suite use the inability to track ROI on social media marketing as pushback as a primary reason for their organizations to not move forward with social media marketing campaigns. I find this rationale pretty thin, and here's why. A number of surveys conducted by different firms, (Lenskold Group, Pedowitz Group, and Sagefrog), revealed that 33 percent of companies around the world do nothing whatsoever in the way of tracking ROI on any of their marketing efforts! Thirty-seven percent don't track the revenue generated by marketing campaigns, 20 percent don't measure the number of sales leads generated by marketing campaigns, and 15 percent don't even qualify leads. Nearly half of B2B companies only track the most basic information like the number of opportunities generated, yet they don't track the number of leads to closed sales. Metrics reflecting the activity that takes place at the bottom of the proverbial funnel should be of great interest to the C-Suite. The most astounding data revealed by the study is that over 55 percent of the Chief Marketing Officers surveyed readily admitted they felt ill prepared to manage marketing ROI.

With the data from these surveys in mind, it's no wonder the C-Suite is reticent about their organization adding a component they don't really understand to the marketing mix. When they state they aren't convinced social media marketing will provide any ROI, their skepticism in understandable. However, a much more accurate depiction of the situation is that the C-Suite at tens of thousands of companies doesn't know the ROI on any aspects of marketing initiatives because of the large number of marketers that don't track it. This seems to explain why well over half of senior-level marketing executives surveyed say they feel unequipped to manage marketing ROI.

Thinking back on the information about metrics, conversions, and attributions from Chapter 9, you can see there is a large amount of data that must be tracked, and it's not easy. It requires a lot of work, but tracking all of that data is required for successful social media marketing campaigns, not to mention for calculating ROI. Choosing not to track any portion of the data forestalls the ability to calculate ROI. If the marketers at a company don't even bother to track the number of leads to closed sales, it's a real stretch to think they're going to track all the data required to calculate ROI from their social media marketing campaigns. Even if marketers don't measure anything, social media affects other channels and should have a positive impact on the bottom line; they just won't know how much.

Authenticity and Measuring ROI

A relevant sub-theme to social media ROI is authenticity – the approach companies' use to connect with consumers has a great deal of impact on the effectiveness of social marketing. Even if a company measures everything discussed in Chapter 9, but engages consumers in methods that are disingenuous, pushy, fake, or indifferent; consumers won't tolerate it, the social marketing efforts will suffer, and the ROI calculations will be skewed. Today's consumers long for transparency and authenticity, and want to know what companies stand for and what ideals they represent. For instance, many consumers will not purchase running shoes that were manufactured in a plant located in a Third World country that uses child labor to assemble the shoes. Consumers want do business with companies that have value systems similar to their own. Factors like the consumer sentiments used in this example impact the ability to accurately calculate social media ROI; even for marketers who are devoted to measuring marketing ROI.

Calculating ROI on Social Media Marketing Initiatives is Difficult; Not Impossible

It is possible to determine the ROI from social media for those who are willing to put forth all the effort necessary to make these calculations. Like all the other important components surrounding social media it must start with strategy. Ascertaining a numerical depiction requires examining the organization's social strategy. However, prior to looking at strategy, organizations must have a clear understanding of where their brand actually is on a continuum regarding the maturity of their social media processes. Organizations in the nascent and secondary stages of their social media endeavors that have just begun to listen, or have been listening and are just entering the learning stage, simply will not be able to calculate ROI yet. The ability to make these calculations takes place further into social initiatives – when the company has gone through the engagement stage, and more so during the stages of analysis and optimization.

Creating a robust social media presence requires an iterative process where progress is continually assessed to be certain the social campaigns are on target. After determining which stage the organization is in with the social efforts, a thorough internal assessment of what the company is doing well and where improvement is needed is essential. A straightforward look at where gaps exist paves the way for creating a strategic plan and tactics that are in sync with defined overarching business objectives. Operating without a strategic plan is a waste of time, money and resources, and impedes the ability to form a model to measure ROI. With a sound social strategy in place and a clear understanding of how to proceed, steps can be taken to correlate variables and their significance for the categorization of ROI.

In addition to being a measurement of money-in vs. money-out, when ROI is thought of as a sequence of events where reliable beliefs are paired with sensible risks, unspecified portions of the strategy increase the risks considerably. Thinking of ROI in this fashion brings about the realization that ROI mirrors strategy numerically.

Getting to the point where the company sees returns on their social media investments requires the same methods utilized calculating ROI in more concrete, tangible parts of the business. Costs need to be calculated for social media endeavors, which include software programs and technology platforms, human resources for the implementation, measurement, management; new processes that may need to be put into place for social integration; and consultants with strategic expertise in the social arena.

Gains need to be calculated as well; and to discover the ROI from social media activities, the gains realized via social initiatives are the ones to calculate. For instance, revenue increases that can be attributed to social media campaigns due to a larger online presence, insights ascertained regarding consumers' sentiments via social media monitoring, increases in brand awareness, the additional generation of warm leads, and the savings from fewer calls into the customer service department.

Since ROI is typically expressed as a percentage, the following formula shall be utilized:

ROI = (Monetary Savings – Monetary Costs) / Monetary Costs x 100(Multiplying by 100 coverts the monetary amount into a percentage).

For example, if the Monetary Savings for a company were $165,250 and the Monetary Costs were $61,400, ROI would be determined thusly: ROI = (165,250 – 61,400)/61,400 x 100 – the ROI = 169%

The primary goal of this book is to provide useful information on social media strategy, marketing, and tactics. Providing an enlightened view includes touching on ROI, and the difficulty encountered calculating social media ROI. By all means, measure everything you can by establishing applicable metrics and KPIs, but when all the information you'd love to have isn't available when it's time to make decisions, those decisions must be made with the information that's presently available. Time waits for no one. The rapidly increasing tempo in which business is conducted today requires companies to constantly look forward and continually adapt.

Return on Relationships

The revenue minus expenses divided by expenses definition of ROI is straightforward in many instances, but using this method for measuring the value of social marketing ROI is challenging. Since this method of measurement isn't an ideal fit for social media marketing, why not look at the value it brings through a different lens? Looking at the value offered by social media marketing, its' positive impact on revenue, and the improved insights all make good sense.

For example, Fan pages on social networks like Facebook are surpassing branded websites for where consumers interact with brands. In fact, the trend many companies are seeing is their brands' social profile is getting more than 10 times as many visits as their websites. Each one of a brand's fans on Facebook is readily identified as an individual who can be engaged in meaningful dialogue. These dialogues provide knowledge – and knowledge is power – the power inherent to these one-to-one relationships is indisputable. Steady increases of the number of one-to-one relationships via these important dialogues is a sure indicator returns are forthcoming.

In Chapter 8 I stressed how engagement with consumers is the desired business outcome that results from actual conversations, meaningful dialogues, listening to consumers to establish trust and develop relationships; and how through those relationships engagements will ensue. All of this is of the utmost importance – the cornerstone of successful social media marketing. However, when it comes to calculating social marketing ROI it's necessary to recognize and admit that the metrics are different and dialogues are not as quantifiable as clicks on Internet banner ads.

Social media has changed the model forever.

Instead of measuring return on investment, perhaps the focus should be measuring return on dialogues, return on engagement, return on brand advocacy, return on relationships; and return on delighted customers voluntarily spreading positive word of mouth and influencing others' purchasing decisions without being compensated for their efforts!

There's a new acronym for you: RODCVSPWOMAIOPDWBCFTE

Social Media Marketing Provides Tremendous Value

Yes, ROI on social media marketing is hard to quantify. However, when well executed social marketing initiatives provide real value and influence purchasing decisions. While those who are excellent at crunching numbers may find this crazy making, forward-thinking companies aren't making the difficulty of measuring social ROI a point of contention. They well know there are significant returns on customer engagement, brand advocacy, and positive word of mouth; all of which are intangible, yet extremely beneficial. The insights gained from persistent listening via social media monitoring enables new knowledge. Making wiser data-driven decisions more quickly is another terrific advantage, yet admittedly difficult to measure. Turning engagements with consumers into dollars is awesome.

While it may seem like a cavalier question when timely highly relevant information facilitates the ability for business executives to make decisions that have an extremely positive impact on the company, is it absolutely essential to drill down into the minutia and attempt to measure the ROI on those decisions right away? Or is it more important to keep pushing on and continually exploit competitive advantages while windows of opportunity are still open? I know from experience what a wonderful feeling it is to steer a company while having the gas pedal jammed to the floor, rocking and rolling, earning business, taking market share away from huge conglomerates, watching revenue soar, earnings increase, and occasionally glancing in the rearview mirror to witness as competitors fall further and further behind – it's exhilarating!

AFTERWORD

Thank you for reading this book and taking this jaunt with me. I appreciate the opportunity to share my knowledge with you and provide insight into the continually changing landscape of social media, online communities, and the strategies and tactics that coincide with this area of business.

It's important to understand where we've been, and look back on the path that led us to where we are at present. Knowing how social media marketing got started and understanding how it has evolved, provides a framework for pondering where social media may go as time marches on. You will be involved in shaping future outcomes as social media proceeds its proliferation within organizations, across industry sectors and around the globe. As you look back on today you may be pleasantly surprised at the influence you had on the evolution of social media marketing.

It's OK to Make Mistakes

Early in this book it was made clear that what is now referred to as social media and social media marketing have actually been around for a long time but were not referred to by these terms. Even so, these practices are unchartered waters for many and that's OK. If social media is new to you, I strongly encourage you to take any feelings of apprehension you're experiencing and turn them into courage so you can blaze a trail. Terms that sound like jargon this week will become terminology that is second nature to you in a month.

Its important to overcome any fear of making mistakes and get started with best practices right away. I can assure you that you're going to make mistakes. Everyone makes mistakes. The mistakes we make give us the opportunity to learn from our experiences so we can adjust our course and keep moving forward. Mistakes are proof we are trying new things – and trying new things based on what we're learning via the social web is wonderful because the status quo simply will not suffice in this global marketplace where business moves at the speed of a Formula One racecar.

It's much better to live and learn via mistakes while trying innovative offering that add value to offering than to sit complacently and become increasingly insignificant to consumers.

Stay on Target

It's important to stay focused on the fact that social media marketing is a vital tool for enabling companies to achieve their key business objectives via the various social network mediums. As results occur your brand enters the spotlight and you start entering into dialogues with consumers on Twitter, for example, fight the "Shiny Unicorn Syndrome" if you feel elated by the intensity of the spotlight. The amplification of your brand and seeing it "go social" is exhilarating resulting in the proclivity to try to do everything at once on every social network to stoke the proverbial fire. By all means get excited! At the same time avoid chasing "shiny unicorns" by staying on target and continuing to work the plan you devised to help attain goals – that help the company realize overarching strategic objectives that lead to competitive advantages, increases in growth, revenue and earnings. Remember, engagement with consumers is the outcome that is preceded by conversations and dialogues about them and their needs.

Resist Temptation

Every company is different. Resist the temptation to compare your social media marketing undertakings to competitors or any other companies. Just because the competition is doing things differently doesn't mean they're doing things better. Considering the overall lack of proficiency about successfully tackling social media marketing, chances are high that your competition is making a number of mistakes – emulating their social activities would be imprudent. Assuming that very large companies or leaders in a market niche are doing everything correctly would be foolhardy. Bigger doesn't always mean better. Blaze your own trail by implementing the know-how you acquired from this book and doing what's best for your organization, rather than attempting to simply duplicate what another company is doing. Have faith in yourself and don't get caught up in second guessing your initiatives just because other companies have chosen different tactics. Who knows if they even have a strategy in place for their social media efforts?

Pace Yourself

Implementing successful social media marketing programs should be a pressing imperative. At the same time please keep in mind this is an ongoing journey, not a 100 meter sprint. While there is a starting block there's no finish line at all.

Yes, there are definite points where a particular campaign will come to an end, yet social media initiatives will remain a key component of marketing going forward. You won't be able to do everything at once so start with a few manageable pilot programs and go from there. As you build muscle and master the execution of the initial projects, you can gradually add other components, and so on.

As I'm sure you've gathered social media marketing is a complex, multi-faceted apparatus with numerous different moving parts. Effectively managing all aspects of the social media machine is a lot of responsibility and requires expertise – developing all that expertise won't happen overnight. Start slowly and pace yourself.

Take the Challenge

A lot of people actually wish social media would just go away.

That's not going to happen.

It isn't a fad, and despite the misconception of many, social media isn't just something 14 year old kids do on Facebook. In fact it's no longer a trend either; so many aspects of social media are rapidly becoming an integral part of business today.

With this in mind I'd like to challenge you to take the knowledge you absorbed from this book along with all the other wisdom you've acquired to champion social media marketing initiatives within your organization. Be the change agent that challenges the status quo by making a strong business case for implementing social media monitoring and Voice of Customer initiatives.

Only the Beginning

Successful social media marketing requires people who are savvy and passionate – people with the right state of mind that not only understand how social media is a highly-effective method for organizations to realize strategic business objectives, but also admit it's a lot of fun! This is my passion; how can I help?

As this book come to an end our relationship is really just beginning. I'm excited about the opportunity to connect with you! My website, StephenMonaco.com is the best way to get in touch with me, and I'm very approachable. I look forward to hearing from you and hope we'll meet in person at some point. Please feel free to call on me if your company needs consulting expertise or has an event in which you would like me to speak. I'd really enjoy hearing how the information in this book helped or inspired you. I'd love to feature successes you've achieved via blogs on my website, and I invite you to share your stories with me.

My Gift to You

While this is the end of this book, it's the beginning of new relationships and we're merely parting ways for now. In the interim, please accept my gift to you: a free bonus chapter of Insightful Knowledge called, "And The Beat Goes On" about the future of social media and other creative uses of social platforms. The additional chapter is available for you to download as a PDF via: InsightfulKnowledge.com/free-bonus

INDEX

ABOUT THE AUTHOR

Stephen Monaco, founder and CEO of Evolve Adaptive Marketing was instrumental in developing online communities back in the days of the BBS and CompuServe; six years before the web browser was invented. In 1987 he was using the strategies and tactics that are now considered best practices for social media marketing. Monaco led Datastorm Technologies from a raw start-up to $50 million in annual revenue. Datastorm experienced 40 consecutive quarters of profitable growth! Stephen's marketing prowess was the driving force behind the world's best-selling PC data communications program of all time, the software mega brand, ProComm, which was published in 11 languages and obtained 70% global market share.

His successful product positioning and pricing strategies from Datastorm Technologies are utilized as examples in the Instructor's Resource Manual for Philip Kotler's graduate-level college text book, *Marketing Management*.

Monaco graduated from the University of Wales – Cardiff, United Kingdom with a Masters in Business Administration with an emphasis in Marketing and eBusiness. The topic of his Masters Dissertation was on the analysis of the impact of the Internet and social media on mass media. Social media marketing is an area Monaco has been researching independently since 1997.

Stephen Monaco works where high tech and integrated marketing intersect – driving strategies and leveraging digital media to effectively realize business goals for early stage ventures, mid-market firms, and large publicly-traded companies.

Monaco is ranked in the Top 25 of the Global Top 100 Social Media Agencies & Consultants for 2013. He is highly ranked as one of the top marketing experts to follow on Twitter. Following his presentation at the Dallas Digital Media Summit in December 2012, @StephenMonaco was the seventh most mentioned name on Twitter during a 3-hour period.

Stephen is a public speaker and has spoken on marketing strategy, social marketing, social media strategy, and entrepreneurism, at corporations, the Kauffman Foundation, colleges and universities, and large industry conferences alongside other thought leaders from Google, YouTube, Twitter, IBM, Dell, PepsiCo, AMD, Intuit, Omnicom, Travelocity, Burson-Marsteller, AOL/HuffingtonPost, Reddit, etc.

In addition to his blog and contributing to the American Marketing Association's "Marketing Thought Leaders" he has written the columns "If You Mean Business" and "Show Me What's Next." His article on social media strategy and listening platforms, "Effective Strategies and Knowledge-Driven Decisions Increase ROI" was republished by Bloomberg / Business Week.

He hosts the weekly one-hour talk radio program, "Rockin' Marketing and Social Media with Stephen Monaco" on the Everything Talk Radio Network. The episodes are of his show are available as podcasts on iTunes. Stephen has been a special guest of the "Panel of Pundits" on the "Silicon Spin" television program hosted by John C. Dvorak, and has been an on-air guest with Rick Dees on the internationally syndicated radio program, "Rick Dees and the Weekly Top 40."

In his early career prior to joining the start-up Datastorm Technologies, Monaco held positions in marketing at Warner Bros. Television - International TV Distribution in Burbank, California, and the corporate communications firm Creative Communications Group in Dallas, Texas.

stephenmonaco.com/bio/
en.wikipedia.org/wiki/Stephen_Monaco
linkedin.com/in/stephenmonaco
twitter.com/StephenMonaco
gplus.to/stephenmonaco
facebook.com/The.Stephen.Monaco

BRING STEPHEN MONACO TO YOUR ORGANIZATION OR EVENT

Stephen Monaco is available for consulting engagements, speaking presentations at your event, and on-site seminars at your organization.

For information on engaging with Stephen, please contact him directly via his website:

StephenMonaco.com

www.ingramcontent.com/pod-product-compliance
Lightning Source LLC
LaVergne TN
LVHW042335060326
832902LV00006B/176